1 MONTH OF
FREE
READING

at

www.ForgottenBooks.com

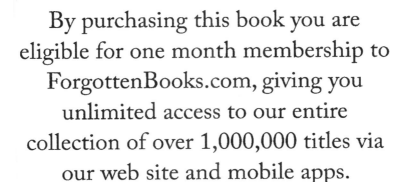

By purchasing this book you are eligible for one month membership to ForgottenBooks.com, giving you unlimited access to our entire collection of over 1,000,000 titles via our web site and mobile apps.

To claim your free month visit:
www.forgottenbooks.com/free1192908

ISBN 978-0-331-48324-6
PIBN 11192908

PROCEEDINGS

OF THE

FIFTY-SECOND MEETING

OF THE

ASSOCIATION

OF

Directors of the Poor and Charities and Corrections

OF THE STATE OF PENNSYLVANIA

HAZLETON, PENNSYLVANIA

OCTOBER 3, 4 and 5, 1927

CHARLES L. HUSTON,
President Association of Directors of the Poor and Charities
and Corrections of Pennsylvania.

TABLE OF CONTENTS

TABLE OF CONTENTS

OFFICERS FOR 1928

PRESIDENT

CHARLES L. HUSTON, ...Coatesville

VICE-PRESIDENTS

T. C. WHITE, ...Mercer
MRS. SUE WILLARD, ...Indiana
DR. J. E. WAASER, ...E. Mauch Chunk
CASPER M. TITUS, ...Philadelphia
MRS. E. C. DUNN, ...N. Glenside
JOHN S. HAMBERG, ...Irwin
S. H. BOYD, ...Columbia

SECRETARY

HARRY A. JONES, ESQ., 522 Washington Trust Building, Washington

TREASURER

D. A. MACKIN, ...Retreat

ASSISTANT SECRETARIES

MRS. J. S. SCHULTZ, ...Ridgway
W. W. DIGHT, ...Mercer

HONORARY SECRETARIES

E. D. SOLENBERGER, ...Philadelphia
T. SPRINGER TODD, ...Uniontown

EXECUTIVE COMMITTEE

The Executive Committee consists of the President, the First Vice-President, the Treasurer, the Secretary, Assistant Secretaries, Honorary Secretaries, the Chairman of the Committee on Legislation and Ex-Presidents, as follows: Charles F. Loesel, (1927), Erie; Mrs. W. Irwin Cheyney, (1926), Media; R. C. Buchanan, (1924), Washington, Pa.

COMMITTEE ON LEGISLATION

Elmer E. Erb, Esq., Chairman, Harrisburg.
D. Glenn Moore, Washington
Major J. Clyde Miller, Pittsburgh
Rodney A. Mercur, Esq., Towanda
W. J. Trembath, Esq., Wilkes Barre

COMMITTEE ON PUBLICITY

A. G. Graham, Chairman, Philadelphia
W. M. Dyatt, Hazleton
George E. Dorwart, Philadelphia
Mrs. Florence B. Cloud, Kennett Square

FIFTY-SECOND ANNUAL CONVENTION
OF THE

Association of Directors of the Poor and Charities and Corrections

OF THE STATE OF PENNSYLVANIA, HELD AT HAZLETON, PENNSYLVANIA, OCTOBER 3, 4 AND 5, 1927 .

The first session of the Fifty-Second Meeting of the Association of Directors of the Poor and Charities and Corrections of the State of Pennsylvania, held in St. Paul's Church Auditorium, Hazleton, Pa., convened at 8 o'clock, Mr. E. J. McKernan, Chairman, presiding.

CHAIRMAN McKERNAN: Ladies and Gentlemen: The Fifty-Second Annual Meeting of the Association of Directors of the Poor and Charities will now come to order.

I will ask Rev. Robert B. Jack, Pastor of First Presbyterian Church to ask the invocation.

... Rev. Robert B. Jack made the invocation at this time...

CHAIRMAN McKERNAN: I deem it a great privilege to have the honor of opening this convention, the first convention of this Association to be held in Hazleton.

The local committee and directors have done everything to try and make your visit pleasant. We hope that you will enjoy yourselves while here and that the meetings will be fruitful.

I believe that Dr. Waaser has a few words to say to our new State President, Mr. Loesel.

PRESIDENT LOESEL: Dr. Waaser, I can't think of words suitable in which to thank the local committee for this beautiful gavel, and I can only accept it with the same spirit in which it has been given. I thank you.

In behalf of the members of the Directors of the Poor and Charities of Pennsylvania, I wish to extend a hearty welcome to all visitors.

We will now hear an address of Welcome from the Mayor of Hazleton, Mayor James G. Harvey.

ADDRESS OF WELCOME

MAYOR JAMES G. HARVEY: Mr. Chairman, Ladies and Gentlemen: I deem this a great pleasure to be here this evening, and to welcome you to the City of Hazleton.

"It affords me great pleasure to welcome to the City of Hazleton, the Association of Directors of the Poor and Charities and Corrections of Pennsylvania. This Association is a real and great accomplishment to help solve some of the public welfare work. The poorer class of people in our communities are in such circumstances by causes unknown to themselves, but a study of conditions will usually prove lack of sympathy and understanding on all sides. The welfare workers could accomplish a great deal if in some way they could teach these unfortunate the essence of the Golden Rule and establish the habit of temperate living and neighborly understanding".

"Their environment is usually depressing where pure sunlight seldom finds a resting place and green growth is impossible. If the poorer people were put in less congested parts of the city where they would have access to play grounds, free parks, and natural beauty, I assure you there would be less crime committed by our juveniles".

"We shall never completely solve the poor problem, but in this epoch of civilization, we can and we must make it easier for the poor to live in a a happy and cheerful environment. Remove the tenement houses, replace them with small homes with a bit of a yard and teach the residents to care for this property in an intelligent way and I'm sure the results will prove beneficial to the community at large. They will have less time to think of themselves and their conditions and they can turn their idle moments into helpful activities, thus occupying the idle mind which generally leads to degradation".

"By keeping these people in a happy frame of mind, utilize their idle moments, and by teaching and practicing the Golden Rule, we shall note a great change among the residents of our cities and boroughs. May you continue to work in your field and accomplish the goals outlined is my wish to you who have been chosen to reduce crime and relieve the poor among us."

"It has been my pleasure to drive down to the place where they say the Poor farm is located. I have driven around what they call the Poor farm. I have looked broadcast over the 900 acres or more of that ground and saw that the management of that farm is being carried out by the right man n the right place."

"I took a walk out to the barn. I am a great lover of animals. I love the animals of all descriptions. I went out to this barn and I saw it all white-washed on the outside. Cleanliness is the next thing to godliness, and while looking at the barn on the outside, after scanning over the land, I passed through into the barn and asked the man to take me through it. I looked around and I must say, without a boast, that the cement floor in back of the cattle was just as clean and tidy as you could possibly make it. And the cattle were standing in straw almost up to their knees. Everything seemed to be in the best of condition.

I saw some of those cows, which were big healthy holsteins, give enough milk to fill a 14-quart bucket at one milking. If those cattle didn't have the proper kind of care, they wouldn't have produced that much milk. Everything was in good shape.

I left that stable and went up to the hog pens. Everything was as clean as could be there also. The floor was as clean, without any exaggeration at all, as the floor at the City Hall. And tomorrow I give an invitation to come up and look at our floor.

I have gone into some people's houses in this locality, and they are not far away. I could pretty nearly throw a stone to the house I have in mind, and I could much better eat from the floor of that pig pen than the table of this house I have in mind.

To bring out what they grow there, they had over 200 hogs in those pens. Just think of what they produce!

I asked Mr. Scanlon, "How is the home financially fixed now as compared to the time when you took hold of it?"

He said, "It costs the Poor district less today, with all of these new buildings here, than it did when I took hold of it".

I used to drive out there when Mr. Gangwere was there. I drive out there once in awhile now, and I want to say that with the new buildings which have been constructed, the new hospital, and all, it is a credit to this organization and the Commissioners who are elected by the people of this district to look after the Poor districts of our community.

And then there are the beautiful drive-ways. I drove by the residence in which Mr. Scanlon lives and around the grounds which surround it. It looks like a villa instead of a Poor farm. It looks like a rich man's palace.

I then took a walk down to where the inmates stay. I spoke to them, for I knew a number of them there. I said, "How do you like this place?"

They answered, "Good, good!"

"You like it all right, do you?"

"Yes, sometimes we have to work pretty good".

I said, "But it doesn't hurt you, does it?"

"No. Mr. Boss, he is all right. Twelve o'clock Saturday, no work until Monday".

And then I asked, "Do they feed you well?"

"Yes, the best. We have plenty to eat".

Ladies and Gentlemen, I never had a man or woman tell me that they weren't contented. And if you or I were left in the same condition as those inmates, I wouldn't want to be placed in a better place than the Poor house.

"Knowing you all to be gentlemen, I herewith extend to you the keys of the city. While in our midst, I know that all of you will be obedient to the law, therefore I wish you each and every one a most pleasant and enjoyable time, while in this Mountain City".

PRESIDENT LOESEL: I heard a little story about Mayor Harvey the other day. He was holding police court and the officer came in about the time that Mayor Harvey got on the bench. "Officer, are there any prisoners today?"

"Yes, your honor, there is one colored man".

"Bring him in."

The officer went out and brought back with him a little fellow about five feet four inches in height, and only weighed about 130 pounds.

Mayor Harvey said, "What are you in for?"

"Ise here fo' lickin' my wife—self protection, boss".

"Officer, is she here?"

"Yes sir, your honor".

"Bring her in too".

The officer went out and came back with a colored woman about six feet tall and weighed about 300 pounds.

"Do you mean to say that you licked your wife on account of self-protection?"

"Yes, boss".

"How long have you been married?"

"About seven months, boss".

"Who married you?"

"You ought to know, yo' married me in yo' office, and yo' did a poor job. Ef yo' ever run for office you will never get my vote".

The next address will be an address of welcome from the Middle Coal Field Poor District, by Mr. John H. Bigelow.

MR. JOHN H. BIGELOW: Mr. Chairman, Ladies and Gentlemen of the Convention: You have been welcomed by the management in charge of this particular convention from the local point of view; you have been welcomed also by the Mayor of the City of Hazleton; and why it would be necessary to welcome you again, I do not know, unless it is to make sure that you are thrice welcome in this district.

This is probably the first time you have met in the City of Hazleton, which is, as you no doubt are aware, a part of the Middle Coal Field Poor District of Pennsylvania, comprised of part of Luzerne County and part of Carbon County. And just why Dr. Waaser, in presentation of the gavel to President Loesel, stated that he gave it to him to remind him that it was 80 per cent carbon, I don't know, but I wish to state that Luzerne should have the credit for we pay about 80 per cent of the taxes.

There was a fellow over there who imagined that he was a great ball player. The world's series now suggests it to my mind. Every afternoon this fellow would go out to an improvised ball diamond and fancy that he was the greatest ball player in the world. He was the star pitcher in the world. He would wind up and he would pitch through the nine innings of base ball to an imaginary batter. And then he would watch the imaginary fielder return the ball, etc.

It was a humorous, and of course a pathetic sight, as all of these matters are.

I met George the night before election, and I said, "How is the election going?"

He said, "Well, I'll tell you. You know, it is pretty hard to fight this time. I have seen all of the people I could, and I have borrowed all the money I could from the bankers—and John, if I am not elected tomorrow, I am going down to Retreat and I am going to be that fellow's catcher."

You folks are engaged in a magnificent work. I know of none which reaches the human heart and human emotions than the department with which you are connected. It is one of the most important functions of government. It might be described to be the "Welfare Department of the Public". The State of Pennsylvania is very careful and considerate of its wards. It has made tremendous strides of progress during the past few decades, and great progress has been made in the solution of all of our social and governmental problems.

There was a time within my recollection when we thought of the Poor house simply as the Poor house, or Almshouse where the unfortunate were committed, where they were only to idle away their time during the last days of their lives until the last great day came unto them to leave this life. They were kept there at the public's expense, and in those days I am sure there was even a more careful supervision of expenditure of the public funds for welfare work than in these days. And you men and women know how carefully the expenditures and appropriations are scrutinized, and how closely the accounts are audited with reference to the expenditures.

The State ought to recognize, and the State has in recent years more so than formerly, the great duty to not only the indigent and unfortuna *l* but the duty and the possibility of maintaining the household in   e, not dissolving and scattering the elements of the family.. They have seen the great need of keeping the family together so that the benign influences of the home and its atmosphere and environment of home life may be given to the children.   Why?   Because the State has an interest not only in the mother and the father indigents, but the State has a greater interest in the boy and girl who are about to ripen into manhood and womanhood and become the future citizens of the Commonwealth.

So it is, in recent years Poor districts and kindred organizations have been given greater power with reference to reclamation and dissemination of help in this regard.   And we, in the Commonwealth, may expect to reap great dividends from this investment the Commonwealth is making under your direction.

I notice that year after year in the Legislature measures have been introduced whereby you are given a more plenary power over matters of this character, and greater discretion in the dissemination of funds.   And the question is raised, "Why?"   As servants of the public you may expect not to be rewarded by praise; you must expect to be made the subject of censure and criticism.   Yet I take it that your greatest reward will be the consciousness of having well performed your duties in a great and sacred occupation to those who are the wards of this State.

In this Middle Coal Field Poor District you will find today a condition that is in striking contrast to that which prevailed with the first recollection I had.

I have no desire to tarry too long and endeavor to paint the picture of the poverty of years ago, and contrast it with today.   I presume you have a reflection of that same condition in the communities from which you all come.

We welcome you to the Middle Coal Field Poor District and we would like to have you visit and observe and see her great resources.   In this district you will find nearly all of the anthracite coal of the world, and yet it is not only of material wealth of which we boast, advantageous though it may seem, but in contrast with these great breakers which you may see, and which are not so beautiful to look at, you will observe close at our door some of the most magnificent rural scenery you have ever had the privilege to gaze upon.   I am not exaggerating at all, and you may think I am something like the fisherman who was fishing along the Wabash.   It was a lovely and beautiful day, just ideal weather for the purpose of luring the bass to the bait.

Over near this fellow there was another fellow who was pulling in the bass about as fast as he could, putting the fish into a basket he had close at hand.

The fellow called to the one catching so many fish, and he said, "How are you doing today?   What is the result of your labors?"

"I have 24 bass and not one is less than one and three-quarters pounds".

And then the fellow said, "Don't you know that it is against the law to catch more than 12 in a single day in this State? Do you know who I am?" And when he said this he displayed his badge indicating that he was game warden.

The fisherman looked at the badge and then said, "Perhaps you don't know who I am. I am the biggest liar in the whole state".

Don't gather the idea because I tell that story that I want to minimize the glories and beauties of this entire community.

I am sure you are all welcome here and sincerely hope that the things along the line of your convention will be pleasant and that much good shall be derived from the meetings which are to be held. I thank you.

PRESIDENT LOESEL: Mrs. W. Irwin Cheyney, of Media, Pa., was to have responded to the addresses of welcome, but Mrs. Cheyney telegraphed that she was unable to be present.

I will call upon Mr. Edwin D. Solenberger to respond to these addresses of welcome at this time.

RESPONSE TO ADDRESS OF WELCOME

SECRETARY SOLENBERGER: Mr. Chairman, Mayor Harvey, Members of the Committee, Ladies and Gentlemen: It has been customary at these conventions that the President of the preceding year respond to the address of welcome, and in that capacity, Mrs. W. Irwin Cheyney, of Delaware County Board expected to be here tonight. In her unavoidable absence, Mr. Loesel suggested that I say a word on behalf of the Convention in response to these addresses of welcome.

Twenty years ago this Fall, when beginning social work in Pennsylvania, I attended my first convention at Meadville. I am not sure that I recognize any one here with the exception of Mr. Mackin who was present at that convention. If there are others here I would be interested in knowing who they are.

Recently, Mr. President, I had occasion to go over the early proceedings of this Association, securing the old copies for binding. I took occasion to glance into some of these old records and while the personnel has changed, and different men and women have come into office, yet the various problems during the 52 years of the life of this organization with which we have had to deal have a very great similarity. Of course we now have different methods of dealing with these problems, but human nature 52 years ago, and human troubles were similar.

In response to the addresses of welcome from the Honorable Mayor and Mr. Bigelow, I wish to say that we are glad to come into the territory of this great and important district, the Middle Coal Field Poor District. We hope that we have brought something to you.

While the numbers of this Convention are not as large as some, we are not here entirely in our personal capacity; we are here in a representative capacity.

The men and women here hold positions in various counties. I c
assure you gentlemen of Hazleton, and of the Middle Coal Field Po
District, that tonight we have some most excellent toastmasters and toas
mistresses. They are doing work in their communities and in their counti
that reflect great credit upon them.

This program has been very carefully prepared, and I wish at this tin
to draw particular attention to the fact that we invite the public to atter
our meetings. I believe that the program will prove to be equally goo
throughout, up to the closing, and we welcome all of our friends of Hazletc
to attend these sessions.

Tonight Mrs. E. S. H. McCauley, Secretary of Welfare, Harrisbur;
will speak to us, and I am sure that we all shall derive a great deal of benef
from her address.

We have arranged a good program and have tried to make it the be;
possible as an expression of our appreciation and gratitude for the wor
that has been done here by Mr. McKernan and the local committee. The
have prepared for your coming and comfort, and as Secretary of th
Association, on behalf of the members of the Association, I wish to than
the people of Hazleton for their kindness.

PRESIDENT LOESEL: It is customary for the President of the Associa
tion to make an annual address, and it reminds me of the story of the mir
ister who had been preaching to his congregation for over an hour and
quarter, when he noticed that Brother Smith had fallen asleep. Rigl
next to him was Brother Brown, who was not asleep but was on the verg
of going to sleep. The minister stopped and said to Brother Browi
Brother Brown, will you please wake up Brother Smith?"

And Brother Brown replied, "Reverend, you put him to sleep and
think it is up to you to wake him up".

I don't think it will take me more than two hours to read this, so try 1
keep awake if possible.

PRESIDENT'S ADDRESS
Charles F. Loesel, Erie

It is meet and right that we should gather here in the beautiful city (
Hazleton this week to get new ideas for the welfare of the people in count
hospitals, feeble-minded homes, insane institutions and childrens homes (
the State of Pennsylvania.

This is the 17th convention of the Directors of the Poor of Pennsylvan;
that I have attended and I find that there has been a great many chang(
in County homes, or better named, County hospitals, I find the old fasl
ioned straw ticks replaced by comfortable mattresses and also find tl
interior painting of rooms is replaced by bright colors instead of dark gree
or dark blue, I also find the food that is given to the inmates of the Count

Hospitals has changed during these years and know that we have advanced with modern times and I believe this is due to the fact that the Directors of the Poor and the Superintendents of these institutions are attending these Conventions and visiting institutions throughout Pennsylvania and exchanging and getting new and better ideas.

We do not want to forget the superintendents, matrons and their employees of these County Hospitals who are responsible for the management of these institutions and I feel that a great many superintendents and matrons are underpaid for the good service that they are giving to the Directors and to the County and the least that we Directors can do when we find that we have a superintendent and matron of this kind is to congratulate them on the way they are taking care of the institution and the inmates and see to it that they are not underpaid for the work that they are doing because they are giving the best part of their lives to this work.

CARE OF CHRONIC T. B.

I find several counties in the State of Pennsylvania that are caring for their first stage T. B. patients on their County Farm. I do not know how successful it is to take care of the first stage patients, but I do believe that the counties should have an institution by itself to care for the unfortunate chronic charity cases.

In Erie County we have tried a chronic T. B. Hospital of 20 beds which, after completion, was filled in 30 days and we now have a waiting list.

It has been the opinion of a great many people that a chronic T. B. Hospital connected with the County Home or County Hospital would not be suitable, as it was thought the patients would object to being committed there due to it being located on County Home property.

There is no chronic T. B. Hospital in the State of Pennsylvania that I know of that cares for private or pay patients. We have quite a number of people in Erie County who apply to us for the admission of their relatives to our chronic T. B. Hospital who would be willing to pay for their care and maintenence.

CARE OF FEEBLE-MINDED

We all know how impossible it is to commit a child to a feeble-minded institution owing to the over-crowded condition.

About two years ago I met Dr. Murdoch, formerly of the Polk State School, at Harrisburg, and asked him the age of the oldest patient we had at his institution. He told me he thought about 62 years old. I asked him on his return to Polk to send us the names and ages of those that he thought could be taken care of at the County Hospital. He advised us that he had six men and one woman which he would exchange for seven children that we had on our waiting list for the past year. This was done and these men and woman are now being taken care of at our County Hospital without any trouble or extra care.

I believe that if the Directors of the Poor would check up their lists they could make many vacancies for children that have been on the waiting lists for a long time.

INSANE

The question of the care of Insane is an important issue with the Poor Districts today.

I find that some counties are caring for their mentally ill in County Hospitals while other counties are sending them to State Hospitals.

Erie County today is supporting about 400 patients in the Warren State Hospital at a cost of about $1,200.00 a week. Our return support is about 20% of the actual cost.

I believe it is the duty of every Poor District to make a thorough investigation of all cases that come under its care to learn whether the patient has any real or personal property that could be applied toward their care.

About a year ago our office was in receipt of a letter from Chicago which stated that they had a man who was mentally ill and a public charge and a legal resident of our County. After confirming his legal residence in our County we committed him to the Warren State Hospital and about a week later we learned he had $9,800.00 deposited to his credit in a Cleveland bank and a guardian was appointed and the County and State were reimbursed and he is now being maintained as a private patient. This man is about 35 years of age, single and a chronic case and likely to live for the next 20 or 30 years.

We also had another case where our investigation showed that a patient had $4900 deposited in a bank in Italy, and after a guardian was appointed, the County and State were reimbursed and then the patient was deported to Italy.

So you can see by thorough investigations the County and State would be saved a great expense.

CARE OF CHILDREN

Last but not least is the question of the care of children.

I do not believe a child supported by the County should be considered as a charity case (in the schools or institutions) due to the fact that all children are receiving their equipment and education on the tax-payers money and these deserted and orphaned children should have an equal footing with the more fortunate ones.

The maintenance of children in private homes, institutions etc., for the year of 1926 in Erie County alone totaled over $15,000.00.

About 20 % of our children that we are taking care of are orphans and about 20% are fatherless children and 60% desertions. I believe we should give them the best of care so they may grow up to be self supporting and a credit to the community and not try to save money, as a dollar invested today will mean 10 community dollars tomorrow.

Our main object for the care of children is to produce self supporting,—better yet, self respecting citizens and to give them something like a fair chance and an even break in the struggle against the odds of circumstances for a place in the world.

When we consider the things that are done that are worth while we are glad to feel that it will make the pathway of life easier for many children, that it will add one more effort for the welfare of the community and bring happiness so we will go on to the end receiving, no doubt, more of a blessing and benefit ourselves than we are able to confer upon others.

There should be better laws passed by the State Legislature for the punishment of fathers and mothers of deserted children and parents who do not give them proper care and food.

I think it was Phillips Brooks who wrote, "The future of the race must go forward on the feet of little children."

PRESIDENT LOESEL: I now take great pleasure in introducing Mrs. E. S. H. McCauley, Secretary of Welfare, Harrisburg, who will speak on the subject, "Work of the State Department of Welfare".

WORK of the STATE DEPARTMENT of WELFARE
Mrs. E. S. H. McCauley, Harrisburg

At the outset may I express to you how much I appreciate having been invited to meet with this group of public officials. I recognize the value of this opportunity to address the assembled members and friends, in this, the fifty-second annual meeting of the Association of Directors of the Poor.

The topic assigned to me is "The Work of the State Department of Welfare." It is very satisfying to know of your manifest interest in the State Department of Welfare. The problems with which the Department comes in daily contact are of great interest to you, because they are co-ordinate with those questions of vital import which from time to time present themselves for your solution.

It is my intention to talk to you tonight, rather than present a formal address. It appears that where there is an interchange of thought the greatest amount of good results from the consideration of problems of mutual interest in an informal way.

It seems desirable to first review with you the history of the creation of the Department and outline its organization so that you may be able to more clearly visualize this subdivision of our State government.

The Department of Welfare was created by an Act of Assembly, May 25, 1921. This was early in the second biennium of Governor Sproul's administration. The Department is, therefore, not quite seven years old. Fifty-six employees are busy in our offices and fifty-nine are employed as field workers. The Department was organized into four Bureaus:

Bureau of Children
Bureau of Mental Health
Bureau of Restoration
Bureau of Assistance

Each has a Director who is in charge of and held responsible for the work in his or her Bureau. Each Bureau is specialized to render excellent service in its field of related activities. The State Council for the Blind is in the Department of Welfare but is not connected with any one of the four Bureaus to which I have just referred. These are co-ordinated under one Chief Executive, the Secretary of Welfare, who, in turn, is answerable to the Chief Executive of the State, His Excellency, the Governor of the Commonwealth.

The Bureau of Children is engaged in the field indicated by its name. It has advisory care of no less than 50,000 dependent children throughout the State. It also has supervision over the administration of the Mothers' Assistance Fund. A special supervisor directs this work. The additional appropriation of $1,000,000.00 by the last legislature to this Fund has enabled Pennsylvania to extend aid to the major portion of that deserving group of children who may thereby be enabled to remain with their mothers.

The Bureau is also concerned with the rehabilitation of crippled children. The 1927 Legislature appropriated $55,000.00 to be used by the Orthopedic Unit during this biennium. Three field representatives render efficient service in this sphere of activity. Since June 1, 1927, nearly one thousand children have been examined and many of this number have been operated upon in the State-aided diagnostic and operative clinics.

The Bureau of Mental Health functions in connection with the proper care and treatment of those who are mentally ill. It also has supervision over the institutions for the feebleminded. The Bureau holds approximately fifty-seven mental clinics monthly throughout the State.

The supervision of the penal and correctional institutions is the work of the Bureau of Restoration.

The Prison Labor Division functions under a Superintendent of its own. Prison industries carry on a business which aggregates annually $900,000.00 in round numbers.

The Bureau of Assistance has supervision over the State-aided and State-owned medical and surgical hospitals; the homes for adults which receive financial aid from the State and the almshouses. The work of this Bureau is, of all Department of Welfare work, most familiar to you who are Directors of the Poor. Mutual interest in the care of the inmates of the almshouses brings you and the personnel of the Bureau of Assistance together in frequent conference.

The Department of Welfare has, as you know, been urging hospital facilities in every almshouse in order that the chronically ill may be given adequate care. Some of the institutions are already equipped to render this service and it is our belief that Directors of the Poor are rapidly coming to realize the need and demonstrating their willingness to provide for such necessity.

These should be, in every instance, institutions which will be a credit to the individual community and to our great Commonwealth. Each one should provide for the needy inmates a county home which is clean, well lighted, sufficiently ventilated, adequately heated and equipped with proper bathing and toilet facilities. Plain, nourishing food should be served three times a day. The Department disapproves, as you know, of a child being born in an almshouse, and consistently upholds the law with regard to children residing in an almshouse. As public officials you and the employees of the Department of Welfare are dealing with a big State-wide problem.

Any organization, if it is to succeed, must have a dominating, impelling purpose which gives life and direction to all its activities. The Department of Welfare is motivated by a two fold purpose — prevention and restoration. The most essential being the work of prevention. Within the memory of most of us the average orphaned child was destined to spend his youth in the orphanage; the adult dependent, however worthy or unworthy he might be, sought comfort in the poorhouse; the mentally ill were taken to the asylums and considered to be hopelessly insane. The criminal "served time" in idleness which deepened his hatred toward the society which would sooner or later become his victim again. But we have come to realize that in so far as it is possible individuals should be saved from becoming either dependent, delinquent or criminal. The institution must be a place of last resort, and always a place wherein and whereby, if possible, the unfortunate can be fitted to be restored to his place in the community.

It is the duty and privilege of every public official to stimulate local interest in this human problem. Lay citizens should be encouraged to visit their county institutions. Their attention should be called to the fact that the question proposed for solution is not only a social one, but economic as well.

We are told by most reliable authorities that dependency and delinquency are rapidly increasing. Is it then not reasonable to inquire where the money is to be found with which, in the future, to finance a problem larger than the one which now presents itself for our consideration? The reasonable answer appears to be the necessary adoption of a possible plan for prevention of rapid increase in dependency and delinquency. The immediate provision and use of sufficient funds will safeguard Pennsylvania's social and economic interests. If this is not done then where, may we hope, will the on-coming generation find the money with which to finance this great work.

Directors of the Poor and employees of the State are mutually interested in the well-advised use of public funds in order that actual human dividends may be the result. Close cooperation insures mutual benefit. Co-operation is the master key which opens the door through which our Commonwealth may walk to prosperity. To us has been given opportunity to work for the "children of our children; for the generations yet to be." We are about to learn that the conservation of normal human life is the greatest contributing factor in the conservation of the world's wealth.

Our united effort in the interest of a great objective, will if pursued, make of Pennsylvania a cynosure for the nation.

PRESIDENT LOESEL: We are all very glad that Mrs. McCauley had a safe journey here, for I know that we would have missed this fine address had she not been able to come. We believe all that she said regarding the cooperation and assistance offered by the State Welfare Department. I think it is up to us to do all that we can and assist in putting over the fifty million dollar bond issue next November.

... The meeting adjourned at 9:30 o'clock...

TUESDAY MORNING SESSION
October 4, 1927.

The second session of the Fifty-second Annual Meeting convened at 9:45 o'clock, President Charles F. Loesel presiding.

PRESIDENT LOESEL: It is time for the convention to come to order We will have the invocation pronounced by Rev. Joseph H. Price, Pastor of this church.

... Rev. Price made the invocation at this time..

PRESDENT LOESEL: I wish to appoint the following committees:

COMMITTEE ON OFFICERS

Mrs. W. J. Trembath, Chairman, Wilkes-Barre.
Mr. R. C. Buchanan, Washington County.
Mr. T. C. White, Mercer County
Mr. A. G. Seyfert, Lancaster County.
Mr. E. M. Lowe, Warren County.
Mr. E. J. McKernan, Hazleton.
Mrs. W. Irwin Cheyney, Delaware County.

AUDITING COMMITTEE

Mr. A. G. Graham, Chairman, Philadelphia.
Rev. P. L. Carpenter, Lancaster County.
Mr. Ira B. Wenger, Franklin County.

RESOLUTIONS COMMITTEE

Mrs. E. C. Dunn, Chairman, Montgomery County.
Mr. Fred Gates, Venango County.
Miss Mary Murphy, Lackawanna County.
Mr. John L. Wood, Greene County.
Mrs. T. C. White, Mercer County.
Mr. G. J. Bruger, Luzerne County.
Mr. George E. Reed, Cumberland County.
Mr. William H. Shirk, Lebanon County.
Mr. Mike Brady, Warren County.
Mr. R. N. Corson, Philadelphia County.

The next on the program will be a memorial for the late H. Wilson Stahlnecker, to be given by F. Kenneth Moore, of Norristown.

MEMORIAL for H. WILSON STAHLNECKER

MR. MOORE: I presume that the older members are familiar with the work done by Mr. Stahlnecker, but the younger ones will not remember him.

Henry Wilson Stahlnecker was born in Norristown, Montgomery County Pennsylvania, on the 27th day of June 1878, and he received his early education in the Public Schools of Norristown, graduating from the High School there in 1895 as president and salutatorian of his class. In the fall of the same year he entered the College Department of the University of Pennsylvania and was graduated four years later with the A. B. degree, having won first prize for sight reading of Greek in his sophomore year, prizes for Greek and Latin in his junior year, and first prize for Latin essay in his senior year. Naturally, as a result of these scholastic activities, Phi Beta Kappa Fraternity elected him to its membership and he later became a Harrison scholar in classics in the Department of Philosophy, receiving therefrom his degree of A. M. in 1900, in which year he entered the Law School of the University of Pennsylvania, graduating therefrom with his degree of L. L. B. in 1903. Having been admitted to the Philadelphia Bar in June 1903 and to the Bar of Montgomery County in July of 1903, he was the first student from Montgomery County to pass the State Board of Law examinations which had been originated in 1901.

Mr. Stahlnecker grasped early a thorough knowledge of the law and became a sound scholar therein as he had done in his studies at college. Due to an impairment in his hearing, his practice was not in the courts, and it was on the business side and as a student of the law that Mr. Stahlnecker stood pre-eminent. Endowed with wisdom, good judgment, integrity, industry and a sound knowledge of his profession, he soon became known and was widely sought for advice.

Mr. Stahlnecker was specially conversant with the Welfare Laws. He acted as Solicitor for the Montgomery County Poor Directors for a period of ten years from 1916 to 1925. During the latter part of his tenure he also served as Secretary to the Board of the Directors of the Poor of Montgomery County. He was also very active and interested in the affairs of the Association of the Directors of the Poor and Charities and Correetions of Pennsylvania, attending all of the conventions and being a diligent and guiding spirit in the Solicitors' Round table meetings and on the floor of the conventions. His thorough knowledge, profound advice and kindly sympathy were widely sought and respected.

He was a good husband, a true friend, an honest lawyer, a sincere Christian, and a thorough-going citizen. With his passing into the unknown, there goes a personality that will not be forgotten, so long as those who knew him still live.

PRESIDENT LOESEL: We will also have a memorial for Mr. Hiram H. Pensyl, to be read by Secretary Solenberger.

MEMORIAL for HIRAM H. PENSYL

SECRETARY SOLENBERGER: Dr. H. J. Sommer, of Blair County sent word that Mr. Pensyl had passed away and that his funeral will be held today. Dr. Sommer has forwarded this brief account of Mr. Pensyl's twenty-eight years of service as Director of the Poor in Blair County.

"At 7:15 o'clock Oct. 1st. 1927, Hiram H. Pensyl, for 28 years and 9 months a Director of the Poor for Blair County, died at his residence in Altoona.

Thus passed a man who was a constant and consistent friend of the Poor—and of the Insane. He was always ready to aid any one in distress. He was consistent in the administration of his office regarding his duties as a Director of the Poor. He had certain definite policies and adhered to them religiously but at all times was willing to be convinced if a change seemed best for the unfortunates and the county at large—always mindful of the needs in any one case and of the institutions under the charge of his Board—he gave his best efforts and time to this work never allowing private business or any other matter to interfere when duty called.

A friend, a helper, and adviser—"a man to tie to"—he will be sorely missed in this Hospital for the mentally ill.

PRESIDENT LOESEL: We have another memorial to Mr. Frank B. Bausman, which will be presented by Mr. A. G. Seyfert at this time.

MEMORIAL for FRANK B. BAUSMAN

MR. SEYFERT: I am not unmindful of the fact that one of our members has passed to the Great Beyond, and it is with a feeling of profound sadness that I appear before you this morning to pay a word of eulogy to the memory of a dear departed friend and intimate, personal co-worker in the cause for which we are here in convention assembled this week.

Frank B. Bausman was a member of this Association for twenty-four years, and attended every meeting that was held during that time. You knew him as an unassuming, modest, attentive listener at all the sessions. He was a quiet worker as chairman of many important committees from year to year, and as such his chief aim was to make each succeeding convention better than the last.

Mr. Bausman came from one of the best known and most prominent old families that settled Lancaster County as early as 1725. Sixty-seven years ago he was born on the original homestead farm located just west of Lancaster on the Millersville pike. The two farms in the Bausman name, as part of his estate, are about one-half of the three hundred and seventeen acres which have been in the Bausman name for two hundred years.

Mr. Bausman was a man of fine physique, as you well remember, due largely to his splendid heredity and outdoor life as a farmer — a stalwart, wholesome type of manhood, developed only from a clean life of generations before. He knew not what it meant to be ill, for he was never sick until a few days before he passed away on September the sixteenth. The uncertainty of life and the knowledge that in the midst of it we are in death, was truly brought home to us in concrete form when we learned that Mr. Bausman had left us for that realm from which none ever returns.

Every now and then one hears the trite and somewhat sarcastic insinuation about political life: "There are few officeholders who die, and none ever resign." This well-worn maxim of political wisdom was certainly hard hit during the past few months in Lancaster county, inasmuch as the Sheriff, one of the Judges of the Common Pleas Court, the Coroner, and a member of the Board of Directors of the Poor have all gone to their last resting place. The latter two were consigned to earth on the same day and at the same hour, just two weeks ago.

Mr. Bausman was elected a Director of the Poor in November, 1903, and took his seat as a member of the Board on the first Monday in January, 1904, from which time he served continuously until his death, with two more years to serve before his full term expired. Twenty-four years is a record that has never been equalled as a Director of the Poor by anyone in Lancaster county or anywhere in the state, so far as I am aware. Mr. Bausman also served his township as school director for more than twenty years. He was a member of the advisory board of directors of St. Josephs' Hospital, vice-chairman of the Lancaster County Children's Aid Society, a member of the Lancaster County Historical Society, and a life-long member and communicant of the Millersville Reformed Church. This is an unusual record of public service for a man who was devoted to farm life.

The welfare of the poor and unfortunate was ever uppermost in his thought. For a quarter of a century he gave the best of his life to make their condition better and happier. They have lost a good friend, and will miss him; so has the Children's Aid Society and this Association. The community in which he lived for nearly three-score years will miss him as a kind, considerate neighbor who was ever willing to be a good Samaritan and devote his time unselfishly for their comfort in hours of distress. He was a most devoted husband and father — the ideal Christian head of a family that loved him dearly. They too will miss him above all others. His friendly, smiling countenance is hidden from us in the narrow tenement of the dead, but in memory's eye we still see it as when face to face we conversed with him. He was a man of high moral attainments, and his standards of life had much of the fundamental ideals of conservatism. In this mad race of existence men of his type are much needed to balance the other extreme. We miss him for that, for the world needs now more than ever in its history just such men as he.

I can only say again that he was a good citizen and a Christian gentleman who helped to make the world better for having lived in it. His mortality has put on immortality, and in the language of his favorite hymn, he is now "Asleep in Jesus."

PRESIDENT LOESEL: I think we were all acquainted with these three gentlemen who have passed to the great beyond, and I believe that a resolution is in order to place these three memorials on the minutes of this convention.

MR. E. J. McKERNAN: I move that the three memorials be spread upon the minutes of this convention.
... The motion was seconded and unanimously carried ...

PRESIDENT LOESEL: I believe that Mr. J. C. Tucker, General Superintendent of the Prison Industrial Board would like to make a few remarks, and at this time we will give him about five minutes.

MR. J. C. TUCKER: Mr. Chairman, Ladies and Gentlemen: I am glad to express at this time our appreciation for the splendid cooperation we have had from you people in carrying on the work of restoration, as we are undertaking to conduct it in connection with our prison industries.

I think you have had this presented to you annually during the last three or four years, and perhaps most of you are familiar with this work. Last evening you heard something about it from our chief, and I am sure as you heard Mrs. McCauley speak you were not only interested in what she was saying, but you were also charmed with her personality and would like to know her better. I want to say to you that we who are working more intimately with her in the welfare work have this appreciation to a greater and more intensive degree.

Mrs. McCauley spoke of our prison industries and appealed to you to support them. The manner in which you can support, of course, is through the purchase or use of the products of Pennsylvania prison labor. The prime purpose of prison labor, of course, is to keep these men occupied and train them for life work in order that they may be able to earn a living upon their return to society, so that they will be an asset instead of a liability.

We may not be able to make them all better, but our experience and our records show that we can accomplish a great deal in this respect. To do all this we must conduct the industries for there can be no training and wholesale occupation unless we conduct them along the lines of the industries on the outside. We set that as our standard, and we have received assistance from both labor and manufacturers. We have brought the standard of our products up to that which compares favorably in grade and quality and workmanship to the products of similar classes on the outside.

To do this it costs money and it requires modern machinery, and also requires more intensive instruction and supervision than the manufacturers give on the outside. It requires more supervisors per man because all of these men come to us untrained. They are raw recruits and our labor must be created from that sort of people.

You can see the quality of our products here which are shown in the exhibit, and you will agree I am sure that we have accomplished something which is worth while.

When a man is doing a good piece of work he can not be thinking of bad things and have evil thoughts. This work has contributed to the discipline of the penitentiaries more than anything else, for it is good wholesome work.

I just want to add a word as to your part and our part cooperatively. I would like to feel and I hope you do, that we all belong to the same big family in this State, people who are undertaking to help these less fortunate. You are using public funds; we are working with public funds. When you purchase the goods manufactured by prison labor, the proceeds are returned again into public funds and do not go into private pockets.

Prison labor has been self-supporting during the last four years or more, and the appropriation which was made at the last administration was turned back. We manufacture these goods not for a profit, but we make just enough to keep the industry self-supporting. I am sure you people will appreciate the importance and logic of circulating public funds in such a way so that they will again function in carrying on some sort of welfare activity.

And so from this point I would like to appeal to you especially, wherever you can possibly do so, make purchases from the Department of Welfare. We have an exhibit out here which covers practically all of our products, with the exception of furniture, and those specimens are too cumbersome to carry around.

Mr. Hogan, our sales representative in the Western part of the State, and Mr. Sherman, sales representative in the Eastern part of the State would be glad to call upon you, giving you any more information that you may desire relative to these products. I thank you.

PRESIDENT LOESEL: Mr. Theurer, our Treasurer, was unable to be present at this convention, and Mr. Arthur Graham will read the Treasurer's report at this time.

(1926-1927)

THE ACCOUNT OF

W. G. THEURER, TREASURER OF THE ASSOCIATION OF
DIRECTORS OF THE POOR, CHARITIES AND CORRECTIONS
OF PENNSYLVANIA
For the Year Ending October 1st, 1927

MEMBERS OF THE ASSOCIATION OF DIRECTORS OF THE
POOR, CHARITIES AND CORRECTIONS OF PENNSYLVANIA:-

I herewith submit my tenth and last report of the financial condition of this organization. I am indeed sorry that I can not be with you in person, but my new duties preclude at this, my busy time. However, my heart and thoughts are with you, and I will always cherish the many good friends and associates I made while engaged in the good and noble work. Keep up the good work and I trust that I might be able to drop in and say hello at many of your future meetings.

Upon the election of your Treasurer for this coming year, I will arrange to turn over all the monies remaining in the Treasury as well as all books and accounts.

I desire to thank you, one and all, for the help you have given me during the past ten years.

I wish to acknowledge receipt of the following dues during the year ending October 1st, 1927.

RECEIPTS

1926		Received from	Amount
Oct.	15,	Kulpmont Poor District	$10.00
"	15,	Guardians of the Poor - Bristol Township	30.00
"	21,	Directors of the Poor - Cumberland County	30.00
"	30,	Directors of the Poor - Erie County	30.00
"	30,	County Commissioners - Indiana County	30.00
"	30,	W. G. Theurer - Washington County	5.00
"	30,	Germantown Township Managers of Relief etc.	30.00
"	30,	Directors of the Poor of Roxborough Poor District	30.00
Nov.	1,	County Commissioners of Bradford County	30.00
"	1,	Directors of Poor - Bloom Poor District	10.00
"	1,	County Commissioners of Clearfield County	30.00
"	1,	County Commissioners of Elk County	30.00
"	1,	Mt. Carmel Borough	10.00
"	1,	Directors of the Poor, etc. - Fayette County	30.00
"	1,	Directors of the Poor, etc. - Perry County	30.00
"	1,	County Commissioner of Warren County	30,00
"	1,	Childrens' Aid Society of Pennsylvania	20.00
"	2,	County Commissioners of Beaver County	30.00
"	2,	Childrens' Aid Society of Somerset County	10.00
"	3,	County Commissioners of Clarion County	30.00
"	3,	Directors of the Poor - Middle Coalfield District	30.00
"	3,	Directors of the Poor of Westmoreland County	30.00
"	4,	County Commissioners of McKean County	30.00
"	4,	Directors of the Poor, etc. - Somerset County	30.00

Forward $605.00

Directors of the Poor of Dauphin County 30.00
Directors of the Poor of Franklin County 30.00
Directors of the Poor - Philipsburg Borough 10.00
Directors of the Poor, etc. - Delaware County 30.00
Directors of the Poor - Huntington County 30.00
Board of Overseers of the Poor - Williamsport 20.00
County Commissioners of Venango County 30.00
County Commissioners of Butler County 30.00
County Commissioners of Jefferson County 30.00
County Commissioners of Potter County 30.00
Armstrong County 30.00
Overseers of the Poor - Lock Haven 10.00
Directors of the Poor - Mercer County 30.00
Board of Trustees State Hospital for Insane -Warren   15.00
County Commissioners of Forest County 20.00
Directors of the Poor - Northampton County 30.00
Directors of the Poor - Washington County 30.00
Overseers of the Poor - Northumberland County . .   5.00
Directors of the Poor - Allegheny County 30.00
Directors of the Poor - Bedford County 30.00
Directors of Susquehanna Depot & Oakland District   10.00
Directors of the Poor - Blakely Poor District 30.00
Board of Trustees - Penn'a. Industrial Relief 15.00
Directors of the Poor - Chester County 30.00
Childrens' Aid Society - Warren County 10.00
Directors of the Poor of Oxford & Lower Dublin 30.00
Directors of the Poor of Montgomery County 30.00
Department of Public Welfare 30.00
Public Charities Association of Pennsylvania 10.00
County Commissioners of Tioga County 30.00
Directors of the Poor - Scranton Poor District 30.00
Directors of the Poor, etc. - Lancaster County 30.00
State Institution for Feeble Minded of Western Pa. .   15.00

Pennsylvania Training School - Morganza 15.00
Directors of the Poor - City of Carbondale 20.00
Directors of the Poor, etc. - Schuykill County 30.00
Directors of the Poor - Montrose Borough 5.00
Valley Township - Poor District 10.00
Directors of the Poor, etc. - Bucks County 30.00
Directors of the Poor - Lehigh County 30.00
Directors of the Poor - Berks County 30.00
Childrens' Aid Society of Western Pennsylvania . . .   20.00

Blair County Directors of the Poor 30.00
Directors of the Poor - Central Poor District 30.00
                                                        _____
                      Forward $1655.00

1927		Received from	Amount
		Brought forward................................	$1655.00
Jan.	19,	Childrens' Aid Society - Westmoreland County....	10.00
Feb.	2,	Directors of the Poor, etc. - York County........	30.00
"	7,	Board of Trustees - Penn'a. T. S. for Feeble Minded Elwyn....................................	15.00
Mar.	19,	Directors of the Poor - Mifflin County............	30.00
Aug.	2,	Directors of the Poor - Lebanon County..........	30.00
"	4,	Directors of the Poor-Cumberland County (1927-28)	30.00
"	31,	Directors of the Poor - Erie County (1927-28).....	30.00
Sept.	17,	State Hospital for Insane - Warren (1927-28).....	15.00
"	17,	Guardians of the Poor - Bristol Township (1927-28).	30.00
"	30,	Over payment on check No. 175.................	4.32
		Total Receipts............	$1879.32

THE TREASURER HAS PAID OUT AND CLAIMS CREDIT FOR THE FOLLOWING DISBURSEMENTS, AS PER THE RECEIPTS ON FILE, DULY APPROVED BY THE PRESIDENT AND THE SECRETARY.

DISBURSEMENTS

1926		Paid to	Amount
Oct.	5,	Arthur Berbracht - stamps for programs..........	13.50
"	6,	C. H. LeBlond - Expenses Cleveland to Erie......	10.00
"	15,	Robert W. Kelso - Expenses Boston to Erie.......	65.95
"	15,	Directors of Poor Erie Co. - Mounting gavel, etc..	10.00
"	25,	Helen M. Booz - Stenographic work - Treasurer's report.....................................	10.00
"	25,	Postmaster - Washington, Penn'a. - stamps.......	5.00
Nov.	1,	Childrens' Aid Society of Penn'a - stamps, etc.....	6.87
"	1,	Edwin D. Solenberger - incidentals..............	1.53
"	2,	W. G. Theurer - Expenses to Erie..............	39.51
"	23,	H. V. Pike, M. D. - Traveling expenses to Erie meeting..................................	40.87
"	23,	Harold Smith Miller - Reporting Erie Convention	142.28
"	23,	Edwin D. Solenberger - Salary as Secretary.......	500.00
"	23,	W. G. Theurer - Balance of Salary as Treasurer...	100.00
1927			
Jan.	31,	Dep't. of Welfare - Prison Labor Division - Printing	15.25
Mar.	19,	Photo-Chromotype Engraving Co. - Cut of Pres...	6.85
"	30,	W. G. Theurer - Part salary for 1927............	100.00
Apr.	28,	W. G. Theurer - Expenses to Hazleton..........	50.00
"	29,	Priestley Printers - Catalogue and envelopes......	9.75
"	29,	R. C. Buchanan................................	45.68
		Forward.....................	$1173.04

		Received from	Amount
		Brought Forward.................................	$1173.04
"	29,	D. A. Mackin..................................	5.00
"	29,	Mrs. Alice Llewellen...........................	30.78
"	29,	E. D. Solenberger.............................	18.61
"	29,	E. J. McKernan..............................	1.00
"	29,	Elmer E. Erb.................................	27.10
'	29,	E. M. Lowe..................................	35.28
"	29,	Charles F. Loesel.............................	48.30
May	21,	Dept. of Welfare-Bureau of Restoration - Circulars	12.75
June	1,	Edwin D. Solenberger - stamps..................	38.00
July	15,	Dept. of Welfare, Prison Labor Division - annual report.......................................	246.50
Aug.	2,	Mrs. Mable H. Fay - folding President's letters, etc.	3.80
"	2,	E. S. Hurff - Furnishing and addressing envelopes.	4.90
"	2,	Groschuff and Fehr - Binding...................	7.20
"	2,	Priestley Printers - folders.....................	58.50
Sept.	12,	Dept. of Welfare, Prison Labor Division - Printing..	3.75
Sept.	12,	Edwin D. Solenberger - stamps and parcel post.....	11.69
"	12,	Groschuff and Fehr - Binding...................	4.60
"	26,	B. F. Barr & Company - Flowers for Frank Bausman	10.00
"	26,	John A. Bayless - Gavel and postage.............	31.16
		Total Disbursements.......	$1783.96

Balance on Hand - 1926.......................	167.12
Receipts During Present Year..................	1879.32
Aggregate....................................	2046.44
Disbursements During Present Year.............	1783.96
Balance on Hand.............................	$262.48

I do hereby certify that the foregoing account is correct and true as stated; that the sums therein mentioned were expended for the benefit of the Association, upon the approval of the President and Secretary.

Respectfully submitted,

W. G. THEURER
Treasurer

We the President and Secretary, of the Association of Directors of the Poor, Charities and Correction of Pennsylvania, have thoroughly examined the above accounts and herewith duly approve the same. All expenditures itemized therein bear our approval.

CHARLES F. LOESEL
President

EDWIN D. SOLENBERGER
Secretary

REPORT of the AUDITING COMMITTEE

We, the undersigned, having been appointed to audit the accounts of the Treasurer, beg leave to report that we have performed that duty and find that there was a balance in the hands of the Treasurer at the time of the last audit in the amount of One hundred sixty-seven dollars and twelve cents ($167.12) and that he has received during the year from Poor Districts, Institutions and Societies the sum of Eighteen hundred seventy: nine dollars and thirty-two cents ($1879.32), making in all the sum of Two thousand Forty-six dollars and forty-four cents ($2046.44).

The Treasurer has paid out, as per his approved receipts, for the usual and necessary purposes of the Association, the sum of Seventeen hundred eighty-three dollars and ninety-six cents ($1783.96), leaving a balance on hand amounting to Two hundred and sixty-two dollars and forty-eight cents ($262.48).

Respectfully submitted,
Auditing Committee

A. G. GRAHAM
P. L. CARPENTER
IVA B. WENGER

PRESIDEMT LOESEL: We will now hear the report of the Committee on Publicity.   Mr. W. M. Dyatt is Chairman of this committee.

REPORT of PUBLICITY COMMITTEE

MR. W. M. DYATT: Mr. President, Ladies and Gentlemen: Mr. Solenberger has requested me, as Chairman of the Publicity Committee, to briefly state what has been done.   I know that you people have important business to take up and a great deal of important work to do, so I will be brief.

We have taken care of the local papers and the metropolitan dailies, seeing to it that the proper publicity has been given this convention.   However, I might say, it wasn't necessary for us to do an extremely hard job because the people of Hazleton were so delighted that you people were coming here, the word was spread around very thoroughly.   I am sure that if you noticed the paper this morning, and also when you see the paper this evening and tomorrow morning, you will agree that the convention will be properly written and properly taken care of.

Mr. Solenberger has also requested me to say something about the Chamber of Commerce work in the city of Hazleton.   I might say that the Chamber of Commerce hasn't done very much in the way of charitable enterprises during the last several years.   Recently through suspensions and the loss of markets, the hard coal business has gone through a terrifying crisis, and this region has suffered tremendously.   Therefore the work of the Chamber of Commerce has been trying to boost the hard coal business in this region.

When Mr. McKernan first broached the subject to us of trying to locate your 1927 convention in Hazleton, we were decidedly glad to cooperate with him, appreciating the fact that it would give us an opportunity to get better acquainted with you and your methods of doing business in your noble work, and at the same time give you a chance to see Hazleton, its environments and meet its people, and to that end we desire to thank publicly Mr. McKernan and his worthy associates of the Middle Coal Field Poor District for their fine accomplishments.

I don't know if I should skip the beauties of Hazleton because the Mayor and the City Solicitor have given you those facts, but I know that you will thoroughly enjoy Hazleton, its scenic beauties and its hospitality, and that you will leave Hazleton with a pleasurable sense of being well taken care of.

I do however want to briefly call your attention to some of the work being done by the Civic Clubs, with a faint idea and a faint possibility of what powerful adjuncts they are along the lines of your work, which is charity.

The Kiwanis Club have been actively engaged in looking after the un-privileged boy. We have sponsored them, have given them assistance through the Y.M.C.A., hold audiences with them every week, and endeavor as far as we can to make real good American citizens out of these boys.

One of our members is an attorney, and recently a young boy was to be sentenced for an automobile offense. The judge was going to send him to one of the reformatories. This attorney said, "Your honor, if you will allow me, as a member of the Kiwanis Club, I will see that this boy is properly taken care of and looked after, and we will try to do what is right."

The judge did this and I am glad to say that this boy today is in a fair way becoming one of the best little fellows you ever saw, and undoubtedly will be a credit to his community as an American citizen.

The Rotary Club has done a splendid thing in the way of the Crippled Children Movement. They have arranged to have Dr. Rau from Phila-delphia look after this particular work.

The Lions Club has done a lot in this city to furnish the poor and indigent with a free supply of milk.

Also the churches and various clubs, and the united charities have done much in the promotion of this splendid work, alleviating misery.

In the coal regions with its large cosmopolitan population, composed of representatives of almost every nation under the sun, we are in a somewhat advantageous position to study racial characteristics as applied to public welfare and charity. We, therefore, feel that by coming to Hazleton you will get a direct contact with the different problems involved owing to our cosmopolitan population which we hope will be beneficial.

For your information, I might also state that we have fully equipped Social Service Exchange, organized for the purpose of preventing unscrup-ulous applicants for charity, sending in duplicate requests.

That, in brief, is about all I have to say. We welcome you to Hazleton, and let me say to you in conclusion that if there is anything that the Chamber of Commerce can do for you, not in connection with the convention, but possibly some favor they could render, something you want done, we will appreciate it if you will get in touch with the Secretary of our Chamber of Commerce.

One thing in particular which struck me this morning was the memorials to these men who have been connected with your organization who have gone "west." What a wonderful attribute to a man's character, to a man who has lived a useful life and a man who has died in the harness doing good for others, leaving this and going to that land where no traveler ever returns. It is fine for those who are left behind to show this respect. I thank you.

PRESIDENT LOESEL: We know that Mr. Dyatt means every word he has said and we all agree that we have been received with open arms here in Hazleton. We hope that we may come back again.

We will now have a report from Secretary Solenberger for the Executive Committee.

REPORT OF EXECUTIVE COMMITTEE

EDWIN D. SOLENBERGER, PHILADELPHIA: The Executive Committee met in Hazleton, April 29, 1927. Present:—Charles F. Loesel, presiding; D. A. Mackin, Retreat; Mrs. Alice Llewellyn, Johnstown; W. G. Theurer, Washington; Elmer E. Erb, Esq., Harrisburg; E. M. Lowe, Warren; R. C. Buchanan, Washington; and Edwin D. Solenberger, Secretary, Philadelphia. Regrets were received from the other members of the Committee who were unable to be present:—Dr. H. J. Sommer, Hollidaysburg; Mrs. Sue Willard, Indiana; Mrs. W. Irwin Cheyney, Media; T. Springer Todd, Uniontown.

Representatives of the Middle Coal Field District and Local Committee were also present by invitation as follows: E. J. McKernan, Chairman; John A. Bayless, E. F. Warner, S. W. Drasher, John T. Scanlon, Supt. District Home, and Mrs. Scanlon, Matron. Also Mayor James G. Harvey, O. C. Whitaker, Miss Ethel May of United Charities of Hazleton; Gertrude P. Keller, Social Service Exchange, Hazleton; G. Stuart Engle, Chairman of Local Committee on Entertainment; Charles Wilde, Percy Faust, and a number of other members of the Local Committees who came in for luncheon.

Under the By-Laws, the Executive Committee is charged with the duty of preparing the program and making arrangements for the meeting of the Convention. With the able assistance of the excellent Local Committee, these matters were attended to except certain details of the program which were left with the President and Secretary. The result of the work of the Executive Committee is shown in the printed program distributed at this meeting.

As the Secretary has asked, on account of pressure of other work that his resignation be accepted at this time, he wishes to record his very great appreciation of the cooperation he has received from the members of the Convention since accepting this office at Reading in 1915.

The Association has grown in numbers and increased correspondingly in influence. Changing conditions in all of our counties have brought new responsibilities and problems to the Poor Districts of the State. It is to be hoped that our meetings may be increasingly successful in helping to bring practical information and light on many problems connected with the work of the members of this Association.

In order that there may be a permanent record for the future, I wish to report that I have made an effort to locate as many as possible of the Proceedings of this Convention from 1876 to date. Louis C. Colborn, Esq., of Somerset, a former President and Secretary of this Association, has contributed some valuable copies. I was also able to find quite a number in the old files of the Children's Aid Society of Pennsylvania, which has been a member of this Association since 1883.

The Library of the Department of Welfare at Harrisburg has a bound volume of Proceedings from 1876 to 1883 and the Library of the Pennsylvania School for Social and Health Work, 311 South Juniper Street, Philadelphia, has a complete bound set from 1884 to date. These two sets make the only complete file that we have been able to locate to cover the entire period of the existence of the Association.

The Library of the Department of Welfare at Harrisburg also has a majority of the copies of the Proceedings from 1885 to date, but a number are missing. Likewise the State Library at Harrisburg has a considerable number of copies from 1881 to date, but unfortunately not a complete file. Your Secretary, after considerable correspondence and search, was able to furnish to both of these libraries a number of copies that they did not have. In addition, partial sets of the Proceedings have been furnished as far as available to the libraries of the University of Pennsylvania, State College, University of Pittsburgh, and the Carnegie Library of Pittsburgh.

Any of the above mentioned libraries that do not have complete sets would be glad to hear from anyone who has old Proceedings or who knows where they might be secured. University teachers and social workers desiring to make a study of the history of the development of the institutions and agencies that have belonged to this Association through the years, find our Proceedings of value. Therefore, it seemed best to make a permanent record of where they may be found.

PRESIDENT LOESEL: The next is the general subject, "Outdoor Relief.' Mrs. Enoch H. Rauh, Director of the Department of Welfare, Pittsburgh was to have presented a paper entitled "Public Relief Methods in Pittsburgh," but Mrs. Rauh was unable to be present. She did however send us her paper, and if time will permit later this paper will be read.

PITTSBURGH DEPARTMENT OF PUBLIC WELFARE
Mrs. Enoch Rauh, Director

The Department of Public Welfare of the City of Pittsburgh occupies a most unique position among the many Poor Boards of this Commonwealth. It does not dispense out-door relief; – an unusual situation.

About fourteen years ago a request was made in concert by the family case working agencies of Pittsburgh to City Council that the then Department of Charities be relieved of the task of investigation and subsidy of all those requesting and requiring out-door relief. After some educational discussion the plan was adopted.

The family relief agencies then took over the investigation of relief under their own supervision, fitting the relief given to a plan made for the rehabilitation of the family. This procedure has worked successfully – each agency had done its work of family reconstruction in accordance with its own policy and many are the families now living on a self respecting, self supporting basis as a result of this splendid constructive work. It has resulted, especially, in the past few years, in a close and sympathetic cooperation between the City Department and the various private "charities". The Department has only to ask that assistance be given and the response is immediate and generous. While this method has been in practice for a decade we receive many applications for out-door relief. They come from the individuals and from those who are interested indirectly and who do not understand the different ramifications of social work. As a result a certain technique has evolved – briefly it is; a short interview for identification purposes; next a generous use of the privately subsidized Clearing House for Charitable Information. If an identification is made (and this is done in 45% of the cases) the registering agency is telephoned and their attention called to the present crisis in the family. The applicant then is either directed to the agency's office or advised to go home where a worker will call promptly. The treatment depends upon weather conditions, the number of children accompanying the applicant and the physical condition of the applicant, as we try to prevent needless trudging from office to office in a humiliating request for aid. It has resulted, in especially distressing conditions, that the applicant has remained at our office and the visitor has been sent from the agency thus saving the physical strengh of the client. In case the family is not identified we notify the agency that is best organized to give the care needed by the applicant and request that a visit be made. Should the family be known to many agencies (and this is a commonplace occurrence) it results often in a case conference of the interested organizations which clarifies the problem for all concerned. In each instance we meet with the most helpful spirit from our agency friends.

Sometimes our good friends and able co-workers – The County Poor Directors – call our attention to a family that has moved over the city line into the county and who are in need of relief. Our usual procedure is to authorize the County to put in emergency relief (for which we have a small appropriation), then to interest one of the relief agencies authorized to work in the county, to take over the burden, thus relieving the County authorities of further obligation. When such a case is reported from some outlying county where it is impossible to have a Pittsburgh or Allegheny County agency take an interest, we authorize relief for thirty days and then the family must either return to Pittsburgh or take care of themselves.

For out-door health relief we have a staff of ten district physicians who are on call for the benefit of the city's indigent. After the physician makes his initial visit his services are augumented gratuitously by the services of a trained nurse from the Public Health Nursing Association. We send daily to the Public Health Nursing Association a notification of all our doctors' calls and the follow up visit is made within a few hours. This has been not only of untold benefit to our busy physicians but also to the family both in a humane and in an educational way.

Transportation is sought of us almost daily. It has never been the practice of the Department to "pass on" anyone either within or without the state without first establishing the residence and obtaining the permission for the return from the Director of the Poor at the point of destination. While we are awaiting the permission the family is cared for either at the Pittsburgh City Home or temporarily with some of our agency friends. Since its inception the Travelers Aid Society has been of great advantage and we are grateful to them for their initial investigations and their many facilities. Often we are able to develop unexpected family resources through their avenues.

During the past year we have been called upon for an unprecedented amount of Pasteur treatment due to an unusual wave of rabies. We have been fortunate to make arrangements with one of our finest city hospitals to administer the necessary treatment and so far we are happy to say, we have not had one fatal case.

In the matter of surgical appliances for rehabilitation which will enable the recipient to become self supporting, may I say that we have a small appropriation for this purpose but we find that the state compensation law has greatly reduced the need for such. We find that most of our applicants are women and children in need of braces, bandages and shoes, who are called to our attention by the private agencies and by the hospital social workers.

While this program has worked smoothly, satisfactorily and happily we cannot foretell what the future may bring. There are a number of possibilities, each one a study in itself. Should there be a merger of the City and County there is a question whether the private agencies will be able to bear the burden of relief, as each year rolls past it becomes increasingly difficult for them to raise the necessary funds to meet their relief budgets. Again if we should sometime have the benefit of a Community Chest we do not know where the obligation might be placed.   If the burden of dependent children now cared for by the Juvenile Court of Allegheny County devolve on the Directors of the Poor, much serious consideration must be given to the solution of this difficult problem.

The sum total of these thirteen years of comradeship with the private charities of Pittsburgh who have most ably administered the out-door relief for our poor has taught us that this most important work must be at all times and under all circumstances cared for by educated, trained, experienced and substantial people with open minds and with a high degree of wholesome imagination for the work to come.   Our experience has not been visionary, it is a fact.

PRESIDENT LOESEL: We are a little behind schedule so we will go on to the next subject, which is "Non-Institutional Public Assistance in Philadelphia."   This will be presented by Mrs. L. M. Roberts, Bureau of Personal Assistance, Department of Welfare, Philadelphia.

NON-INSTITUTIONAL PUBLIC ASSISTANCE
IN PHILADELPHIA
Mrs. L. M. Roberts

It seems unfair for me to speak on this subject for Philadelphia as a whole because this is not the subject which I was originally asked to discuss and I did not know that it had been changed until after the printed program was issued.   I felt somewhat dismayed at the change since I realized that it was then too late to consult the officials of the six independent Poor Districts in Philadelphia for information on which I might present to you a comprehensive picture of procedure in handling outdoor assistance in Philadelphia.   Therefore and of necessity I have confined my consideration to the types of outdoor assistance in that large district which is called the City of Philadelphia.   It comprises all of what part of Philadelphia lying west of the Schuylkill River, Manayunk, and skirting the lower boundaries of the 22nd, 42nd and 23rd wards, extends southward to the Navy Yard at League Island.

In all of this populous territory our Bureau must be prepared to secure such non Institutional Public Assistance as may be needed by individuals seeking aid or brought to our attention by other persons.

The work of our Bureau falls naturally into two main divisions, namely, that of assistance to families and individuals in distress and the supervision and care of the children who are wards of the City of Philadelphia.

The persons assisted may be classified under the following headings:

1. Dependent families of persons sentenced to imprisonment.
2.   "   "   " the unemployed.
3.   "   non residents.
4.   "   widows not receiving Mother's Assistance.
5.   "   aged or infirm.

6. Feeble minded persons in need of Institutional care.
7. Foundling children.
8. Deserted   "
9. Lost   "
10. Non resident   "
11. Children committed by the Court.
12.   "   of Prisoners.
13.   "   returned by public officials.
14.   "   whose parents are ill.

The procedure employed in discharging the various services required follows the usual case work method of inquiry, analysis and treatment, bearing in mind the fundamental provisions of the Poor Law and paying particular attention to the establishment of legal settlement in order to fix responsibility for pecuniary aid. In other words as public officials practicing social service, it is our duty not only to determine what action should be taken but also how and by whom it should be taken. It is a question of what, how and who.

Such then briefly is the layout of the job of our Brueau — a rather staggering task when one considers that very little money is appropriated for the discharge of these services with the exception of the maintenance of dependent children.

I have been thinking in terms of outdoor assistance other than material relief, the topic which was originally assigned to me.

This is a very interesting topic to those of us who are charged with the administration of Relief under the Poor Law of the State because it immediately lifts our minds from the more prosaic items of food, clothing and shelter to the less tangible social values which may glorify our efforts in the discharge of our duties.

This topic does not suggest the idea that there shall be no material relief nor that other assistance is to be offered in lieu of material relief. As a matter of fact few of the cases with which we deal can dispense with that factor for the reason that we represent the rock bottom in charitable aid insofar as our clients are concerned. Other sources of assistance have been tapped before we are consulted. The fraternal societies, religious organizations and private charitable agencies have drawn off those whom they desire to aid leaving for us that large remainder lying outside the range of their activities or beyond their financial resources.

In connection with this fact I am reminded of a statement which Dr. Richard Harte made in an address at the luncheon to launch the program for rebuilding the Philadelphia General Hospital. Dr. Harte was at that time Director of the Department of Public Health and Charities and as such he was the actual head of that great hospital. He also had other hospital affiliations and, speaking as an insider, he had no hesitation in stating that the private hospitals took the cream of the cases and in his opinion they would continue to do so. But that fact he thought presented no argument against tearing down the antiquated impossible old buildings in which the hospital was housed and erecting in their place an up to date modern hospital adequately equipped to serve that larger section of the people who must turn to the Public for medical aid. He was right. The splendid men who have succeeded Dr. Harte in that great office have pushed ahead along that line and today we see the hospital raising it's wonderful new buildings on its historic site. Who can gaze upon them and doubt, that in the future those who enter its portals for treatment will be able to have the best medical care that can be offered anywhere in the world. A large opportunity presented itself which was met with a vision far flung and which called for large expenditures of public money to be raised by taxation. The taxpayers would have to decide the question. No program of petty economy could be submitted. It must win on the idea of adequate service alone, on results which could be obtained, on the settled conviction that a man's a man for a' that. This it seems to me, is the angle from which we who administer out-door assistance should view our work. To its prosecution we should bring the most approved social service thus far developed. I believe the day has come when we too should offer to our public, to our taxpayers, the vision of a worth while service and results which shall justify their support.

It seems unnecessary to point out to you the supreme importance of the family, for our whole social structure is built upon it. It is the place where every child should receive his fundamental education, where his habits are formed, where his health is established, where his emotions may have an outlet and where the ideas of his relation to GOD and his neighbor take form. We are learning to place the proper emphasis on the importance of the early years in the life of every individual — nay more — to include those months before his birth when his whole existence depends upon that of his mother. We are also beginning to value mothers at their true worth — not from the sentimental point of view — though that can be justified — but from the point of view of productive wealth for while she and her brood may seem to consume wealth, in reality she creates it. And not only does she risk her life in the enterprize but she spends her life in developing it. Her service to her children is one that can not be duplicated — that cannot be bought. For her there are no scheduled hours of labor, no time clock to punch, no vacations with pay. Her's is a twenty four duty and it lasts for years. A baby's cry, a cough, and she is wide awake, on her feet, hastening to see what is wrong. I do not overdraw this picture. I am speaking with restraint for if I were to sketch in the details every person in this room would wrap his head in a mantle.

Need I say more in emphasizing the importance of the family and the duty laid upon us to preserve it, to develop it, to enrich if possible the life of every member of it?

Our method must follow the familiar formula of inquiry, analysis and treatment. In other words we must evaluate the factors and we must have an objective. You will remember that when Solomon was called to be King over Israel he was profoundly affected by the magnitude of his task and by a sense of his own unfitness. It possessed him waking and sleeping and in his sleep he had a dream in which Jehovah appeared and said to him 'Ask what I shall give thee' and Solomon, conscious of his limitations asked for just one thing, that he might be given an understanding heart so that he might deal justly with the people. The record goes on to say that the speech pleased the Lord that Solomon had asked this thing instead of all the material blessings he might have asked for himself. And his request was granted — he was given a wise and understanding heart. This was well pleasing all those centuries ago and we can be sure that an earnest desire to understand is well pleasing at this day, and, since we cannot lay claim to wisdom, our understanding hearts must base our conclusions on facts which must be patiently gathered together and studied. I know of no other way which is safe and sound in theory and practice.

We must learn to interpret facts, to draw the correct inference. A few days ago a charming six year old boy whom we have placed in an adoptive home called to pay his respects. I was occupied and had to ask the prospective adoptive parents and the child to wait a few minutes in the hall. When at last I could see them he remarked that a little boy waiting in the upstairs hall was very happy. 'Why do you think so' I asked and the instant reply was 'Because he sings'. Swift and sure was his interpretation of a fact. And he gave to me a picture of his own superior ability which I believe will be confirmed in his approaching mental examination.

In thinking over types of assistance other than material Relief which may be utilized to conserve and develop the family we find them falling into groups such as Religious, Educational, Recreational, Health, Domestic, Science, Work, Legal Aid and the Courts.

To illustrate the point I have been making, I shall present an example of a piece of work carried out under the limitations set by the Poor Law and which called for a wide range of service.

The case is that of Mrs. X and her five children suddenly called upon to face a crash worse than widowhood. The husband and father, a man of forty-four had been convicted of involuntary manslaughter and sentenced to undergo an imprisonment of sixteen months. The case was referred to us by the very able lawyer who had defended the man. Our investigation showed that the family had always been highly respected in the neighborhood in which they had lived. The man had a good work record and had been a good husband and father. He had occasional lapses from sobriety and while intoxicated he struck a man down and killed him from concussion of the brain due to striking his head upon the curb. There was no doubt about the fact and his attorney was glad to have so light a sentenced imposed.

Mrs. X. was forty. She was an excellent mother and had been a good manager. The home tho plain was neat and clean. There were no debts but also no savings — this last accounted for by the fact that several years earlier all of the household effects had been destroyed by fire and this calamity was followed by the mother's long illness from rheumatic fever. The relatives were all poor and unable to help. Mrs. X. immediately set about helping to keep her family together by doing washing and ironing. Our visitor noticed her shortness of breath and arranged for an early examination at a heart clinic. Here it was found that she had a definite Mitral Stenosis and should do no work at all. The lesion may have been caused by the rheumatic fever but it had been greatly aggravated by the grief and worry over the husband's misfortune and the plight in which her children had been left. The children ranged in age from six years to fifteen years. She was especially distressed about the two older girls fifteen and thirteen years of age and in the second and first year high school respectively. The girls were attractive, bright, ambitious and were planning to become stenographers. She feared it would be necessary to take the older girl from school and place her at work. · To give up the girl's cherished plan seemed like an added calamity. The doctor in charge ordered Mrs. X. to bed for a complete rest as the condition of her heart was so grave that she was in constant danger of dropping dead. We had a heart to heart talk with her, made her see her importance to her children even tho she could do nothing except direct them and we promised to give her $15.00 per week on condition that she follow the doctor's orders. We determined that the older girl's ambition should not be sacrificed if we could help it though with an incapacitated mother it was impossible to make ends meet on our money grant. We therefore submitted her case to the White Williams Foundation for a scholarship and while it was under consideration we secured supplemental aid from the Alliance of Catholic Women.

The White Williams Foundation granted the scholarship and later we were delighted to receive a report from them recommending that after graduation this girl should obtain a position as stenographer or bookkeeper and should be encouraged to take a secretarial course, such as is offered at Drexel Institute.

We called on the Board of City Trusts to provide coal, on the Red Cross and the Alliance of Catholic Women for clothing and in addition our visitor made a personal gift of suitable clothing for the girls in High School.

The twelve year old boy soon became a conduct problem. His mother was much distressed to find that he was deceiving her and was becoming downright dishonest. He had a paper route which he sold to another boy and then collected money from the customers which was due the other boy. There were other instances of dishonesty and when confronted with them he calmly and stolidly admitted every offence and seemed entirely unaffected by being detected. He was in the 6th A grade at school and had been greatly distressed when he found that his father was in prison especially as other boys had cruelly taunted him about it. We arranged for his examination at the Neuropsychiatric clinic at the Pennsylvania Hospital and their study revealed that his delinquency was the result of a sense of inferiority which had developed because his father was in prison. We felt that this child's plight presented a legitimate reason for trying to secure a parole for his father and we took it up but found it impossible to do anything until the minumum period required by law had been served. Failing in this, we enlisted the aid of the Big Brothers Association in the treatment of the child. We saw to it that a generous Xmas basket and gifts for all found its way to this household.

At last the prison doors swung open and Mr. X. was finally paroled. In anticipation of this event a job was waiting for him secured from a previous employer and when the oldest girl graduated we secured work for her also.

In this history we present the picture of a family saved intact. The returning father who never had been in trouble before could take up his life where he left it and while in prison he at least was cleansed of the curse of drink. The mother's life was saved. The record notes one deviation from the rules laid down when she tried to do a little cleaning. It was never repeated for she had a terrifying heart attack. The education of the girls proceeded without interruption and the boy who was developing delinquent tendencies was reclaimed for useful citizenship.

But this happy result did not come by chance — it was due first to a sympathetic understanding of the problem, second to perception of the threatening ultimate disaster to this family and lastly to a determination to utilize necessary measures to prevent that disaster. Suppose a little inadequate relief had been put into this family without that more vital service? What would have been the result? First the oldest girl would have been snatched from school to earn a few paltry dollars and her whole future would have been wrecked. In quick succession would have occurred the mother's death, the disruption of the family, the placement of the children in institutions, the boy probably in the Protectory, the furniture and household effects gone and the family life destroyed.

This case, it seems to me, proves the claim that material aid alone without the vision to preserve, to develop and enrich the family life is worse than useless.

PRESIDENT LOESEL: The next on the program is ":Confidential Registration of Relief Cases," which will be presented by Miss Gertrude P. Keller, of the Hazleton Social Service Exchange.

THE CONFIDENTIAL REGISTRATION
OF RELIEF CASES
Miss Gertrude Pardee Keller

Whenever there is more than one social agency working in a community, certain principles must be adhered to if the best results are to be obtained. Cooperation is essential and this must involve a willingness to discuss mutual problems in order to give families the best service possible and to avoid unnecessary duplication both in effort and relief. In a very small town this is a comparatively simple process. A plan must be made for the widowed Mrs. Smith. The children's school teacher calls upon the pastor and both then talk over the problem with the Poor Director. A satisfactory plan is arrived at. But in a larger city, this problem becomes complex. What agencies have been helping Mrs. Smith? What have they already done and what still remains to be done? The teacher cannot call upon 20 or 30 organizations to find out all the information necessary.

It is at this point that a Social Service Exchange bridges the difficulty. It acts as a clearing house for all welfare and social agencies. The technical part of the Exchange is merely a card catalogue in which are registered the names of all families and individuals known to every organization whose purpose is to help adjust the individual to his environment. The card on which a family is registered is a simple affair. It contains no confidential information, only such data as will help in identifying the family, together with the names of all agencies interested. For those who use the Exchange, the process is very easy. John Brown goes to the Salvation Army with a hard-luck story and asks for clothing. The Salvation Army call up the Exchange on the phone, giving the name and address, and if the man is married, any information about the children's names and ages which will help to identify him. The Exchange, by means of an address file, a name file and a system of cross references, can give the report back in less than a minute. They tell the Salvation Army that the man is known to the United Charities, and to the Poor Board. From these agencies, the Salvation Army learns that John Brown is already adequately provided for financially. Duplication is avoided. An extra investigation on the part of the Salvation Army is eliminated and the pauperization of John Brown has been checked. And possibly after talking over the matter with the other agencies, John Brown can be put upon his feet, for in joint conference, the three agencies may be able to get at the root of his trouble.

But although the avoiding of duplication in giving material relief, is a very important function of the Exchange, it is not the only one. Even more important is the fact that thru it can be brought about a pooling of knowledge and a cooperation which will result in the best plans being made for a family's future. Like a card catalogue in a Library, the Exchange can only point to the place where the information can be found. Each agency must then confer with those already interested and these case conferences mean that no longer will several organizations work at cross-purposes not knowing what the other is doing. They will work together efficiently, throwing light on each other's problems. For the whole story. must be known if a family is to be helped intelligently in helping themselves. The report of the Mental Clinic will help the truancy officer, the results of the pastor's contacts will help the case working agency, and every agency which knows a family must make its contribution of knowledge.

The main rules which organizations using an Exchange must follow are: Inquire immediately. Register systematically and accurately. Confer with agencies already registered and then cooperate intelligently or withdraw gracefully.

The Hazleton Social Service Exchange was organized during 1926 through the cooperation of sixteen welfare or social organizations. Representatives from these agencies met in a joint conference and unanimously voted on the organization of an Exchange. A budget for the first year was drawn up and divided among the member agencies according to the approximate case load of each. The budget was very low as the Exchange was housed in the Red Cross Rooms and had the part time use of their stenographer. Now that the cost of initial equipment has been met, the yearly running expenses are still lower and each agency using the Exchange is charged $10 annually.

The sixteen charter organizations covered a large range in the scope of their work. Family Welfare Work was represented by the United Charities; both public and private relief giving agencies joined, the Poor Board and the Mothers Assistance Fund, and private benevolent organizations, such as the Elks, the Eastern Star and certain Catholic Clubs; organizations helping ex-servicemen or their families; the various service clubs which sponsored any welfare program; certain industrial cooperations; health organizations such as the Hospital, the Red Cross Visiting Nurse Society and certain of the Clinics, and other miscellaneous organizations such as the Salvation Army, Y.W.C.A., & Travelers Aid, and the Chamber of Commerce.

Hazleton's Exchange has still far to go. Last year, there were 331 agencies using the Philadelphia Exchange. These included agencies of the classes mentioned above as well as certain schools, who thru it were able to get information about problem pupils; the Court; Playground; the Employment Department of the Bell Telephone Co., and any organization which includes in its program social or welfare work.

A survey of the use of the Exchange by public agencies in Pennsylvania, shows that in certain cities, the following public organizations cooperate: City School, Juvenile Court, City Hospitals, Bureau of Police, Post Office, State Clinics, Board of Health, Mayor's Office, Probation Officer, State Welfare Department, Children's Aid and Mothers Assistance Fund.

Counties in Pennsylvania in which the Directors of the Poor are registering their cases in a confidential Exchange are Delaware, Montgomery, Allegheny and Berks. There are still others in which the Directors are cooperative in giving information when asked to do so, but do not register regularly.

Here in Hazleton, the Middle Coal Field Poor District was one of the first organizations to sponsor the movement. Because of the large number of families which come to them for help, it is particularly necessary to get as much diversified information about them as possible. Needless investigations are often eliminated because data can be gotten from another agency which has already made a thorough study of the situation. This not only saves time and money for the Poor Board, but also prevents the family from an influx of investigators, all of them well meaning, but making it particularly hard for the sensitive family to tell it's troubles so many times over. Money is also saved because certain cases are cut off the lists when a complete history is gained. The maximum service is obtained for the family. Especially at Christmas time through the special basket exchange, overlooking and overlapping are avoided.

A common objection raised is that an agency's records are private and it would destroy the confidence of the individual to register his name in such a charity file. The answer is that the Exchange is not a charity file. It is a social one and not a blacklist. Families registered are ones in which there is some social problem. It may be a financial difficulty, a domestic situation, or even a temporary health problem. There is no stigma of worthiness or unworthiness attached to the name of those registered. Then too, information on the cards only identifies. It gives nothing of problems or difficulties in the family life, and thirdly it is an absolutely confidential exchange and the records are strictly private. The inquiring agency is merely directed by the Exchange to those who have had previous relations with the family. In case conference it is left to the workers to talk over their own cases.

Furthermore, the Exchange never dictates policies. It will be glad to call a meeting of several of the agencies at the request of anyone, but does nothing regarding the handling of the cases. It acts only as a convenience or short-cut, not as a supervisor, and its ultimate success depends largely on the agencies using it.

In summarizing the purposes of an Exchange, we see it functioning first and foremost with the best interests of a family in view, safeguarding its welfare and avoiding conflicting plans for treatment and care. Secondly it helps the social agencies of a Community to understand each other and to know the service each can give. Thirdly, it avoids unnecessary duplication of effort and means a saving in time and money to the Community.

PRESIDENT LOESEL: The next will be "Cooperation between Public and Private Agencies," and we will ask Mr. O. C. Whitaker to present this.

COOPERATION BETWEEN PUBLIC AND PRIVATE AGENCIES
O. C. Whitaker, Hazelton

I have been asked to discuss the subject of "Co-operation between Public and Private Agencies." Co-operation is a word used almost daily by nearly everybody without giving much thought to just what the act of co-operating really means. Webster defines the word first, "concurrent effort or labor"; second, — "collective action in pursuit of the common well being." Co-operation therefore if it means anything at all, means labor and collective action.

To labor well in any collective action, harmony and loyalty among the laborers must prevail and to these ought to be added the qualities of congeniality and kindness. In the common action, the labor as between Poor Boards and the hosts of private agencies within our State, should be collective. The public has a right to expect harmonious co-operation between them because, in the end, the public pays the bill for the work both are engaged in.

There may be some essential differences between the methods used by public and private agencies in dealing with their common problems, altho the desired result is the same. By collective action can this result be most quickly achieved, for the work of both agencies at times overlaps or dovetails by reason of the nature of the problems that are presented.

As is the case with the public agency, private agencies do not need to seek out cases for their daily work. Enough folks with all sorts of miseries and troubles call daily in numbers quite sufficient to keep the working staffs busy. Warm hearted co-operation between both agencies is the only remedy to keep this number of clients within bounds.

Occasionally private agency workers find that out-door relief is very necessary to help some families regain a normal position in the community and therefore recommend it to the public agency. At other times, because of accumulated knowledge showing that a family's status has changed, the same agency will as freely advance reasons for the removal of a family's name from the out-door relief list. This kind of co-operation reduces the evil effects of pauperization.

Because of being always on the job, the private agency is besought to do much needed social service work that would otherwise have to be undertaken by the public agency or else be left undone, — perhaps to the discredit of the community. This fact is not always realized and appreciated as it ought to be.

To be a real, vital force then, co-operation must be mutual and genial without which it can be chilled and the path of approach to progress be made very difficult.

Because of many personal touches with the family life in a community, it is not too much to say that the private agency is the best ally the public agency can have. One outstanding reason for this may be found in the fact that private agency investigations are as thorough as it is possible to make them, and are not usually the result of a single family visit. The family history and record sheets of the private agency are being constantly added to as future visits and events develop, from the knowledge of which it is often possible to place a family on a self sustaining basis. While these integrating records are strictly confidential, they nevertheless are accessible to any agency having a legitimate interest.

Too much emphasis cannot be placed on the subject of complete investigation of the clients who appeal for help. Skilled investigation affords the means for determining the causes of distress and points out the best way to assist in its relief. A surgeon would be denied his right to further practice if he applied soothing liniments to a broken leg and made no effort to set the broken bones.

The pauperizing effect of duplication of relief can be almost entirely a-voided by intelligent use of the Social Service Exchange. Communities which do not have this proven necessity to welfare work will find that it pays for itself many times over in the expenditure of labor and money. Social Service Exchanges are evidences of community co-operation.

Not all persons applying for aid require material things such as food, raiment, or coal. At times medical, dental, or optical attention and per-haps legal advice are needed; at other times the understanding advice, which a real investigation discloses is the real need in helping to restore normal living conditions.

Co-operation implies labor, — not talk. Discussion without action makes no progress; is like a good clock that is not wound up. I beg to bring to your attention a serious subject, — mental deficiency, — that is perhaps the major cause of poverty and unhappiness in family life and perhaps one of the most costly to the taxpayer.

None are better qualified to grapple with it than the public and private agencies. Their collective action could humanely relieve society of one of its worst destroyers. A news item of Sept. 17, 1927 quotes the gover-nor of New York as saying that a new hospital for the insane will be need-ed every two years in that State at a cost of $5,500,000 for construction alone at the present rate of new patients being admitted, which number has been two thousand annually for the past decade.

These annual conventions of yours are evidences of a desire for co-oper-ation. Our responsibilities are like our shadows; we cannot escape them. It is likely true that "Fools rush in where angels fear to tread," never-theless I want to enter a strong plea for initiative action by this convent-ion in effort to stave the tide of feeble-mindedness which is assuming a-larming proportions.

Not all can agree on how this scourge of humanity can be combatted. It appears to be a disagreeable subject to many who ought to take active interest to the extent of doing more than discussing it. This evasion of action may be due to the enormous size of the problem and its various ramifications.

Segregation is the most talked of solution and perhaps has the most proponents. In Pennsylvania it is estimated that there are from twenty to forty thousand feeble-minded who should have institutional care. If this be true it would require the building of a city approximating the size of Hazleton to house them, to which would need be added the huge cost of maintenance.

Objections can be raised against this method of depriving an individual capable of some earning power of his or her liberty, whose chief offense is the procreation of undesirable progeny with constant regularity.

I firmly believe that if the Poor Boards of our State inaugurate the movement and request the co-operation of the private agencies a bill can be gotten through our next legislature which will make the more humane method of sterilization of definitely feeble-minded people compulsory. Sterilization, we are informed, is not a serious operation and patients quickly recover, possessed of all former attitudes towards life — lacking only the power to reproduce. Should this day happily come then will our present institutions of mercy for such care become monuments to the ignorance so long endured.

Such collective action could also successfully resist the proposed Old Age Pension scheme, resembling the iniquitous English dole system, and which would virtually relieve family responsibility and cast it upon the public. This co-operation could also be of sufficient force to insure the success of the proposed $50,000,000 Bond Issue of which we shall hear from other speakers.

In closing may I repeat that co-operation means ''collective action in the pursuit of the common well-being." Let us prevent, so far as possible, the need for care and questionable cure of human wreckage. Public and private agencies are specialized workmen on that great building, the American family, and we perform a most important part in its structure.

PRESIDENT LOESEL: We were to have had with us today Mrs. Martha J. Megee, of the Department of Welfare, Harrisburg, but Mrs. Megee sent a message stating she was unable to be present.

We will then go on to the next. Mrs. Alice Llewellyn, Director, of Cambria County will now give us her experiences.

MRS. ALICE LLEWELLYN: Mr. Chairman, Friends of the different Districts of the State of Pennsylvania: I believe this morning we are here gathered together for one great cause. To my mind that great cause is the cause of humanity.

As the program states we are to speak on the lessons from experience in giving outdoor relief. To my mind this is the greatest proposition that we directors have to contend with. It not only means handing out a few paltry dollars or a store order to relieve distress. That is all right and is absolutely necessary in most cases, but there are many other things to be looked after besides the material aid which we are giving to the unfortunate.

In this State I believe the average is 225,000 children born in a year, and thousands of those children come under our supervision. Now what are we going to do with them? Are we going to allow them to be raised up with the thought that charity alone will take care of them? Will they be good citizens of tomorrow if they must always have the idea before them that they have been raised on charity? No! I believe we directors after we have made an investigation, and have helped in a material way, we should follow that investigation with frequent visits and see if we cannot better their home conditions.

I have in mind two families which are just the opposite, who are residents of one little town in Cambria County. The one woman was deprived of her husband, he being killed in the mines. She had a little property left to her, and she had five children. There was a mortgage of $600 on this property. While she was receiving the compensation of $12 per week, she could not find a way in which to raise these children and keep them comfortably, at the same time raise the money with which to pay the mortgage.

One of the citizens of that town appealed to me. I felt that I could do nothing more than take up the case with the Board of Compensation, which I did. After explaining her case to them, they came to my aid and asked me to bring the woman to meet the referee. And the referee, after having a conference with this woman and myself, decided that this mortgage should be lifted. They granted her the commutation of the $600, and I want to say to you today that she is one of the happiest mothers we have, because she can now see her way clear to keep her family together.

The other case was a family which I have been laboring with for three years, trying my best to keep them together. The former speaker touched upon the subject most vitally, because had I been granting the marriage license, there would have been none.

The husband and father is a nervous prostrate, and during the last 15 years has been unable to do anything, and yet he had been allowed to marry a woman who had been an inmate of our own County Home. As a result of this marriage two dear little girls were born. I have been working with the family, trying to keep them together until finally the mother (who has a lacking somewhere) was not capable of rearing those two little girls. She became sick and she appealed to me to take her away. I took her to the County Home and also took the children. The father wouldn't go. The children were placed in the Children's Home.

The father stayed, thinking that he and a half-sister could keep house together. As a result they were not getting along for this half-sister was an immoral woman, and the citizens appealed to me again. The only thing to do was to go and break up the home entirely. This I did. I also took him to the County Home.

After the wife had been there less than three months she became physically able to work. I secured a position for her in a family of three, an old lady who I knew would take care of this woman. I want to tell you, today the entire family is taken care of. While I had to separate them, yet I felt I was using the best judgment in the case. The father is now in the County Home and the mother is earning her own living, and the two children are in school every day. They are also being sent to Sunday School, and some day will be a benefit to that mother, because the father cannot live long.

Last year when I spoke to you I also told you about a little girl that I had taken into my home, and I told you that I would tell you this year whether or not it had been a success. I wish to say that it has been a success. I still have that little girl in my home. She is now past 17 years of age, and her Sunday School teacher told me the other day that she is one of the best students she has in her class in Sunday School.

I leave it to you, whether it is worth while to study human nature and see if by our aiding just a little bit, getting away from the financing end of it, if we can't do just a little more in aiding our families who come under our supervision, and what we call our Outdoor Relief. I thank you.

PRESIDENT LOESEL: I consider that a very good talk, and I know that every one has appreciated it. We can all learn a lot from it.

The next speaker will be Mrs. Florence B. Cloud, Director, Chester County.

MRS. FLORENCE B. CLOUD: Dear Friends of the Convention: I am allowed five minutes and I think three minutes will be ample.

In Chester County we have no investigator. Cases are reported to us and almost immediately we investigate them, unless we know the party who has reported the cases. If the information comes from one of our community nurses we know generally who this nurse is and what her investigation has been. We will probably then send her what she has asked for, and in that way help her.

We have worked shoulder to shoulder with our worker of the Mother's Pension. Before these widows were able to get their pension we have stepped in and kept the mother and her children together, and our aim has been to keep our families together if we possibly can.

I have in mind a case where the father was sent to prison for a term, and the mother was left with five children, three of them of school age. The community took care of them through the lodge which this father belonged to. I believe it was the Masonic lodge and they kept the family for quite a long time. Finally the family was turned over to the Directors of the Poor.

On our farms we have several vacant houses, which were comfortably fitted, and we removed this mother and five children to one of these homes. The home was a comfortable four-room house with bath. We did the laundry for her, with the exception of the babies' wash, which we allowed the mother to do. We took her provisions, and she was allowed to do her own cooking and keep house. We fitted the children out for school.

When the father came out after serving his sentence and returned again to the community, we kept that family for two months longer, expecting him to get a job. The Masonic order secured employment for him, after which he took his family to a home where they are now living today.

I have in mind a case where a friend of mine called last week about a man who had lived in that community during all his life. He had no family but a family there had given him a home. Finally the head of the family died and left the widow so that she was unable to take care of this old man. The man is now past 80 years of age. He had had a stroke and is simply helpless.

This woman was left the home, but no income other than what she receives by acting as assessor of the township. She is perfectly willing to take care of the old man if she had a little help. I was asked what we would do.

I told this friend of mine to bring the subject up with the Board of Directors the next day, and as a result the community nurse goes there and does her part, and we donated a certain amount to this lady so that she could take care of the old man. Through it all we aim to keep the children together and if the mother is not able to take care of the children we have a Chester County Children's Aid Society, and I think Mr. Solenberger will stand back of it.

PRESIDENT LOESEL: That also was a very good talk.

While we are waiting for Mr. Trembath, is there anybody who wishes to ask questions? We can have a little discussion here, and probably can limit each one to two minutes in order to give every one a chance to say something.

SECRETARY SOLENBERGER: Most of you will recall that last year we had such a big program in the morning session that it left little time for discussion. I would like to suggest that this is the time now for discussion, and you should now take advantage of this opportunity. We should have some discussion on this subject of Outdoor Relief, and we would like to hear from the members who have something to contribute on this general subject.

MR. CASPAR M. TITUS: I have been interested in all that has been said this morning and I feel now is the proper and fitting time for the various directors from the various institutions where they are elected to serve the people and look after the welfare of those particular institutions to say something. I think in this way we can assist one another.

You must remember that each one has a different idea of doing things at these institutions, and if they will just get up and tell something about what they are doing it may be of benefit to some one in another locality. Each Director has a different way of doing things and I think this subject should be thoroughly discussed, Mr. President.

PRESIDENT LOESEL: I see Mr. Charles L. Huston, of Chester County, and I would like to ask Mr. Huston to make a few remarks at this time.

MR. CHARLES L. HUSTON: Mr. President, Ladies and Gentlemen: I am very glad to greet this convention. I haven't been so long in this capacity, but it might be of interest to make just a few remarks at this time.

My father was a very busy iron manufacturer, retiring from the practice of medicine on account of the fact that his health wouldn't stand it. My mother wanted him to give his attention to the public welfare work. He hesitated to do that, but finally he yielded and accepted a place on the Board of Public Charities.

He came from the southeastern part of the State where most of the people come from Quaker stock, and all of my antecedents were members of the Society of the Friends.

Well, my father accepted the call to become a member of the Board of Public Charities, and the morning that he was getting ready to attend a meeting, dressing in silence as Quakers usually did, my mother said, "Well, Thee is going to the Poor house today, is Thee?"

He said, "Yes."

And then she said, "Well I hope you will find yourself in the right place."

He went into that work and was very much interested in it. One day while he was visiting the jail, and as he passed one of the little windows a voice called, "How-do-you-do, doctor. You ought to know me. I was named for you."

My father didn't know who it was, and finally he gave him his name. This fellow had gotten into trouble for getting drunk and beating up his family. My father asked him his name, and also asked him what he was in jail for. He replied that he was there for abusing his family, and said it just as cheerfully as you please.

This institutional work is the thing, as has been said here, and we should all cooperate. I am interested in the relief of indigent cases, outside of being Director of the Poor. I think it is very important to make a study of the needs of the people. I know that over there near us at Coatesville the people are great for marrying and raising large families, populating the neighborhood with feeble-minded children. Something should be done for it seems to be on the increase. Solutions have been proposed which I think are worth while, but the difficulty is in drawing the line—to know where the effective cure should be made, and where they should be allowed to go on as usual.

Certainly, as interested citizens in a Christian community we should look after those who are unfortunate.

I am very glad to say that Mrs. Cloud, who just preceded me, has made the investigations and has traveled over the county at a good deal of trouble, spending her time and energy. A great deal of credit goes to her. I think it is a splendid place for women on the Board of Directors.

Mrs. Cloud was elected to our Board, and at the end of the first meeting she said, "I am a little surprised. I expected there was going to be a scrap."

I said, "We don't come here to scrap, we come here to attend to business." I want to compliment Mrs. Cloud, not only on her diligence, but for her keen insight and discrimination in looking into these cases, and deciding what should be done. We have no hesitation when she comes to make her report, for we adopt her recommendations without qualification. I think that women, with their intuition and ability to see the inwardness, and ability to investigate the circumstances of the family, can do this work much better than men.

As you know women are on the Welfare Boards, and connected with private organizations, etc., and through their cooperation a great deal has been accomplished. I know that you have the same thing happen in your communities that happen in ours with regard to these dependents trying to work the sympathetic heart and pocketbook, moving from one section to another in order to receive relief. Perhaps they will move away for awhile, and then return, thinking that perhaps you will take care of them again. They get to be professional rounders, and they sometimes will double up in a community, and will receive relief from two or three people.

Through the cooperation of these different agencies the correct information is obtained, and those people who are in need can be helped much more intelligently and their children can be brought up in the proper manner, and in the end the community is benefitted.

I am very glad to be here again. I haven't been at many of the conventions, but I come when I can. I drove over from the northern part of the State, about 100 miles away, and I feel that I have been repaid for the journey.

I don't know that I would have stayed so long in this work, but my wife is interested in it. While I am engaged in the official business with the other Directors, she gathers the people together and holds a regular gospel meeting. The people who have charge of them testify that the attitude of these people has changed and their lives are much better. They are not so quarrelsome, but are kind-hearted, helpful and sweet tempered. There has been a wonderful change in that respect.

Therefore, I say to you who have wives who are interested in that sort of thing, take them with you when you attend your Board Meetings. I thank you.

PRESIDENT LOESEL: I am glad that you came Mr. Huston, and hope that you will stay throughout the convention.

We have with us Mr. William Hill, of Philadelphia, and I would like to have him come forward and make a few remarks at this time.

MR. CASPAR M. TITUS: I would just like to say a few words, ladies and gentlemen, at this time. Some of us men are getting old, and this gentlemen happens to be one of our new Directors.

MR. WILLIAM HILL: Mr. Chairman, Ladies and Gentlemen: It has been said that if you are invited to the banquet and take a back seat they will ask you to come forward.

Being a baby director in our District, I consider it a compliment to be called before you. Really I haven't any prepared speech, and I am not accustomed to making speeches.

I have tried to listen with interest this morning to the prepared speeches and talks, and sometimes I think to myself, like that great man of happy memory to Philadelphia, and not only to Philadelphia, but the entire country, and possibly the world in general—the late Russell Conwell. He often said that there were two kinds of poor: God's poor, and the devil's poor. If you give one dollar to one man, he will buy bread either for himself or his children; if you give another man one dollar he will buy drink, and probably set fire to his home, and if he has no home he will set fire to his neighbor's home, and the conflagration he starts will cause a whole lot of trouble.

That is one thing that we, as Directors of the Poor, have to decipher. We must determine which are God's poor and which are the devil's poor. We are all creatures of God and we are all here through His making, and we must think and look deep into our hearts before we say, "This man is entitled to what is right", or "This man is not entitled to help."

Abraham Lincoln, as you know, said that God loved the poor people for that is the reason that he made so many of them.

Often times we may, in thinking that we are just a little bit better, forgetting that we are the same kind of creatures as the poor unfortunates, say that this fellow is there because of his own misfortune, that he could have done better. But when you go to these institutions, how many do you find who have had the proper chance in life, but some one has tripped them up, and things didn't just go the way they had intended?

I am glad to be a member of the Poor Board, and I will try to do my work with a feeling that I am trying to do what is right. I really think that of all those who are intrusted with public funds will stand up and do the work they are entitled to do, the work they should do, and not allow any one to point a finger at them that they are using those funds for a way other than they should be used for, then the poor will be properly taken care of, for there are many instances where men are put in trust to take care of the needy whereby they misuse the appropriations. I thank you.

PRESIDENT LOESEL: I am glad that Philadelphia elected a young man in the office of Poor Director. I know that he is interested in the work. I always like to see the young man come out for Poor Director, and if he likes the work I like to see him stay in the work, because he is bound to make a success. It is folly for an old man, a man past 60 or 65 years of age to run for these offices. I think it is a young man's job so that he can grow up with the office.

Mr. Trembath is now here and I will ask him to speak to us at this time.

MR. W. J. TREMBATH: Mr. Chairman, Ladies and Gentlemen: The Sunday School teacher said, "Mary, do you know a scripture text?"

"I'll say I do!"

"All right, Mary, tell it to me."

"The Lord is my Shepherd—the Lord is my Shepherd—I should worry."

The first part about the shepherd I think we will refer to Rev. Mr. Carpenter, who is always in attendance, for further consideration and deliberation. The "I should worry" part I think is a very appropriate text for a congregation of people like this, the members of the Poor Board. And the Lord knows that we have plenty to worry about. I just want to direct your attention to one subject which has worried me for years.

For the information of myself, as well as yourselves, I have made an analysis of the last 100 cases which have come under my observation, for the purpose of ascertaining the cause of the distress. Here are the results:

Out of the one hundred cases, 33 were due to widowhood. That is to say, in some way or another the breadwinner was taken away, leaving the widows and dependents families to the mercies of the Poor Districts.

I have classed 34 as disability, that is injuries, sickness and accident.

Two are due to insanity of the husband, and three to prison sentences. Three I classed as general shiftlessness, which might be called low mentality; two for lack of work.

That leaves 23.

Those that I have designated up to the present time I think falls in with the thought of the last speaker from Philadelphia, and might be termed as God's poor.

Before coming to the remaining class, I will give you the further analysis of one of the two main classes so far referred to, namely widowhood. They may be summed up as follows:

21—disease (various kinds.)
5—mine accidents.
2—miner's asthma.
2—tuberculosis.
3—old age widows.
—
33

Those which come under the disability cases may be summed up as follows:

12—disease (various kinds.)
6—mine accidents.
4—other injuries.
4—old age.
5—miner's asthma.
3—tuberculosis.
—
34

I call your attention to the fact that the total number, out of the 100 that are charged up to the main industry of this neighborhood is 18. They are as follows:

5—mine accidents.
2—miner's asthma.
6—disability cases from mine accidents.
5—   ”   ”   ”   miner's asthma.
—
18

That makes 18 per cent charged to the chief industry of this neighborhood. Of course they are entitled to relief. The whole of that group so far may be called God's poor because they make out an untainted claim to the charity of the community, particularly those suffering from miner's asthma. They are entitled to maintenance from the cost of the industry.

Now the 23 out of the 100 cases are not God's poor. I think there is a partnership between God and the devil there, as far as the women and children are concerned who are left behind. They might be under the protection of the diety, but how about the fellows who run away? There is where the devil takes a hand in it.

There are times when the father, during hard times when the mines are not working, will run away. And then when investigarion is made, the wife can easily say to the Poor Director that she is left alone with the children, and the Poor Director cannot say that she has an able-bodied husband in the house and that he is able to earn a living for them. He will perhaps stay away until there is work again and then will return home. This occurs very often when there is a strike, and then after the strike the miner will return. It is a clever arrangement and entirely within the law. However those desertion cases are not so well known in your localities. The desertion cases do not run as high as 23 per cent. The husbands in your localities are perhaps more careful of their responsibilities. There might be an excuse for an occasional deserter.

I knew of a fellow who married a widow with six or seven children and then the production went on until he reached 12 or 13.

You may find these desertion cases in the coal regions in the western part of the State. They were the cause of considerable thought to the Commission to Codify and Revise the Laws relating to the Poor Districts, who a few years ago attempted to codify the Poor laws. I don't know if this proposed remedy will appeal to you, and I haven't tried to work it out.

There was an Act of 1876 which defines "Vagrancy". Your codifiers added one more definition and that reads as follows:

Sec. 1, Act of May 8, 1876, P.L. 154 (with paragraph V added.)

V.   "Husbands who shall desert or refuse without reasonable cause, to maintain and support their wives or family."

And you will find that it gives authority to the Directors to issue a warrant and apprehend and convey or cause to be conveyed to a justice of the peace or other committing magistrate of the county, and commit him to the custody of the steward, keeper or superintendent of such county farm, house of correction or Poor House.

You can commit him to not more than six months to the Poor Farm, which for the purpose of the enforcement of that act is classified as a workhouse by the act, and they work him on that farm and hire out his services for revenue. The earnings of the able-bodied deserter, whether paid directly by the Poor Board, or somebody else, will defray the cost of the maintenance of the deserter's family, at least in part, and at the same time reimburse the district.

You will find that the difficulty is that the ordinary Alms or Poor House has no means for restraint, no confinement, nothing to prevent the man imprisoned under the provision of that act from running away at his own sweet will.

That has been provided for, at least the attempt has been made to give an opportunity to provide for that particular matter through the construction of buildings or enclosures.

As I say, it is an untried remedy, and I am merely calling your attention to it. You will find it under Section 1100, of the Report and Recommendations of the Commission to Codify and Revise the Laws Relating to Poor Districts and the Care of the Poor. There you will find that method of taking care of the deserter who is not entitled to any sympathy, and the only other element in the solution of the problem, of course, is the most important one—the recipe for making rabbit soup; first catch the rabbit.

However, they do come back, and I am certain that if that remedy is tried out, and the noise of it gets abroad, it will reduce the percentage of desertion in my district below 23 per cent.

I thank you.

... The meeting adjourned at 12 o'clock ...

·ROUND TABLE NO. 1.

TUESDAY AFTERNOON SESSION
October 4, 1927

The meeting convened at 2:45 o'clock, Mr. John T: Scanlon, Chairman, presiding.

PRESIDENT LOESEL: It gives me great pleasure to introduce to you Mr. John Scanlon, Steward of Weatherly, who will take charge of this session this afternoon.

CHAIRMAN SCANLON: We will now open the round table session, and I will ask Mr. Mackin, Superintendent of Retreat, to make the introduction.

MR. MACKIN: This marks the fifth year of our Round Table discussions, and I think that you will all agree that the inauguration of this type of meeting has done much to make our conventions both interesting and profitable—as for myself, I always look to this discussion for practical suggestions and have never been disappointed.

The program, this year, I find especially interesting and practical, and I am interested in hearing the view points of the various members of the meeting in regard to the subjects, that to me, seem of vital importance in the administration of our institutions.

I am most interested in hearing suggestions in regard to diet in our County Homes. The question of variety in the diet, particularly at seasons of the year when vegetables are at a premium, and the preparations of foods for the sick are two important problems.

We are so situated that we are not called upon to deal with the tramp, but the vagrant problem is one that we all have to contend with, and Dr. Henderson and Miss Martin will probably have interesting experiences to relate on this question.

From the discussion on administration of the County Homes, I expect to find many practical suggestions that I can apply to my own institutions. Mr. Halpenny, Mr. Todd, Mr. Coombs, and Mr. Scanlon have had such success in directing their homes, that I know they have many suggestions to offer.

The topic to be opened by Mr. Holcomb is one that is commanding considerable attention throughout the country. The institutions have been under fire by certain organizations and individuals, and they make no distinction between those homes which are mismanaged, and those that are advancing to meet the needs of modern times. If the County Home is to be eliminated, what is to be done with all of those patients that we have under our care?

The question of old age pensions is one that is being agitated in our State at present. What will be its effect on our County Homes? Will it be sufficient to keep the old people in comfort? Mr. Seyfert and Mr. Buchanan will give us their views on this subject.

The subject of training courses for nurses and attendants in County and District Homes, which I have been asked to introduce, is one that, at present, I am vitally interested in.

The necessity of having trained people to care for the chronically ill is too apparent to require any argument. The problem, however, of finding Registered Graduate nurses to devote their time to this type of institutional work is a difficult one. Speaking from my own experience, I have found it practically impossible to find a nurse to take a night position. When we decided to specialize in work for the chronically ill, we established a standard of employing only graduate nurses, registered under our State law. Notwithstanding the fact that we offer a salary equal to that paid by other hospitals, it seems impossible to keep the positions filled. I am interested in the subject, and hope to get some ideas from the discussion. Personally, I believe we must have the general hospital train our nurses if we are to maintain a standard that will command the confidence and respect of the public.

CHAIRMAN SCANLON: I will now call upon Dr. Ralph L. Hill, Woodville, Allegheny County. (Not present)

I will then call upon Dr. M. C. Yeager, of Mercer County. (Not present)

Dr. Waaser, wouldn't you like to give us a little talk on this subject "Training Courses for Nurses and Attendants in County and District Homes with Special Reference to the Care of the Chronically Ill?"

DR. J. E. WAASER: Mr. Chairman, no doubt I would like to give you a talk, but frankly I don't feel I would be qualified to talk as intelligently on the subject as these men who have been assigned the subject. The very few words I will say will be more or less scattered. I won't talk to use up time.

Mr. Mackin's plan at Retreat is one that undoubtedly should be followed up by every institution. Practical nurses are very splendid people and in the majority of cases they answer the purpose and fill the bill, but there is a percentage of the cases occurring in these public institutions which absolutely demand the service of nurses who are skilled to the point where they are able to register and be approved by the authorities of the State.

Perhaps I could best illustrate that by telling you that in our own institution we have well taken care of the situation, and have been during the past three years. We have a trained nurse who is well qualified, and to those of us on the directorate who have had the opportunity to compare this service with a service which was perhaps equally efficient, we notice a very decided difference.

There is a feeling of security that comes to those in authority, and the condition of the patient is materially benefitted.

This is a subject that is dear to me to talk about, and I wish that I had had a little notice so that I could have pulled the subject together and presented it to the convention. I thank you.

CHAIRMAN SCANLON: We will call upon Dr. I. A. Freyman to say a few words at this time on the subject.

DR. I. A. FREYMAN: This is a man's job and I am not equal to it. I haven't prepared anything on the subject and will have to ask to be excused.

CHAIRMAN SCANLON: I will now call upon Miss Ranck, Head Nurse, Westmoreland County. (Not present)
Are there any other nurses in the room?

MR. D. A. MACKIN: Mr. Chairman, this is a subject in which I am deeply interested, and it seems a pity that it should fall by the wayside. I wish some of the members would just relate their experiences in regard to this matter. I know there are a lot of institutions which can't afford to engage registered nurses, as the rates are too high to pay, etc., but let us discuss it.

With regard to our own institution the daily average will be 400, with a maximum of 500 during the winter. From the statistics gathered from the medical examinations, 96 per cent are ill, suffering from some definitely diagnosed disease.

We have adopted a plan, and have established a standard of having only the graduate nurses, approved by the State, and of course the proper number of orderlies. This can be done, perhaps, in an institution of the size of ours, but when you talk of operating a hospital the general hospital superintendent would smile at operating a plant the size of ours with the small personnel we use. However, they don't understand that we draw and train our orderlies from among the patients. We have three paid orderlies, so the graduate nurses have ample assistance to train their patients in all of the work.

I would like to hear from some of the other institutions and see how they get along.

It is very hard to find trained and graduate nurses to stay in the work. It isn't that the work is too hard, but it isn't quite as interesting as the general hospital work or the work of a private nurse. And again it is 12 months in the year.

We have tried to make our conditions as reasonable as possible. Our salaries are on a par with those paid in the general hospital for permanent workers, but yet we have that problem in trying to keep those positions filled.

I had hoped that some one would tell me where I could get two graduate nurses. Two positions are now open at Retreat.

DR. WARREN Z. ANDERS: Mr. Chairman, with reference to trained nurses, the home with which I am connected engages practical nurses. We have had experience with trained nurses, and after we have them a little while, they say that they are not learning anything, that it is the same kind of work. They leave us and then we must fall back on some good practical nurse whom we know.

With regard to attendants, our institution is located but 25 miles from Philadelphia and we are in a good position to secure rather good attendants. Most of them have had experience in some good hospital. If we could get a trained nurse to stay with us we would make some inducement for her, but we don't seem to be able to hold them, since I have been in the position during the last 12 years.

CHAIRMAN SCANLON: I wish we could hear from some of the matrons present.

I would like to ask Dr. Holland to speak to us if he will.

DR. W. E. HOLLAND: I am from Franklin County, half way between the town in which I live and Chambersburg, and when we have any surgical work, we simply move them into the hospital. We don't have much use for a trained nurse. Our cases are all chronic and we have a couple of men from Philadelphia who have had plenty of training. We pick out certain ones in the women's department and train them if needed.

I thank you.

CHAIRMAN SCANLON: . I wonder if we could not have some discussion from the matrons or superintendents present.

MR. P. H. BRIDENBACH: I am from Blair County, and with reference to the nurse proposition, I want to say that we are fortunate enough to have a trained nurse, and we find that it is a paying proposition to the County.

In our institution we have 122 inmates, and out of those 122 we have 14 bed patients. About four or five of these patients have sore limbs and this trained nurse must dress these three or four times a day. I don't think that a practical nurse can give the attention to the patients that a trained nurse can. It seems to me that the trained nurse can find the dirty holes in the institution and try to keep the place looking clean, more so than the practical nurse.

I have only been steward at the County Home for six months, but I have been brought up with the work practically all my life. I was seven years with the Ford Motor Car Company as special investigator among the employes, where there were 72,000 employes in one factory. Our work was to see that they had the proper kind of living conditions after they had been with the company for a period of two weeks. There were about 80 per cent who were foreigners and they didn't know how to live.

From my previous experience, I would say that what you want if you can get them are trained nurses. We pay our trained nurse $80 per month, including board, etc.

The inmates were sitting on their beds there on account of lack of room, for in the winter we have around 160 or 170 inmates.   Mrs. Megee came along about the time we had proposed to make more room for them, and she said that while we were going to build a sun parlor we might just as well put on another story, making it into a sick ward.   It is going to be a fine thing.

We have about 40 women, and the rest of them are men.

CHAIRMAN SCANLON: In my estimation, no one can do this work unless they are trained and paid for it.

DR. J. E. WAASER: We are obliged to leave this round table and hold our own, but there is just one thought that occurred to me from the remarks I have heard during the last few minutes.

Very naturally and properly this matter of getting the best of nursing ability should be paramount for the sake of the patient.   But looking at it from a practical and economical viewpoint, I would like to stress the fact that it certainly does pay a Poor district to have a professionally trained nurse, and by that I imply skilled.   They are able to do a great deal of the work that would necessarily fall to the lot of the attending doctor, with all probability of added expense.

A well trained nurse, aside from the dressing of ordinary chronic wounds is well qualified to take care of many of the medical ills, if I may so call them, which in itself would be of much benefit to the patient, far better than having a few stock bottles—this for "cramps"; this for "vomiting"; this for "headache", etc.

My experience has been that these skilled nurses are just about half-doctors.   And as I said before they are a great benefit to the inmates.

MR. T. C. WHITE: I am not a doctor, nor am I the son of a doctor, but I have had some little experience.   I have been very much interested in the discussion this afternoon.

I think there is a place for the trained nurse, but I haven't found the place for her in the ordinary County Home.

My experience has been that when you put one in, you drive the practical nurses out.   The two will not work together.

If you place a trained nurse at the head of the insane ward, then you lose your practical nurses, but if you can secure a nurse that has been instructed and trained in the mental hospital, then you have one which will meet the requirements.

When you ask the trained nurse to go down to the Home among the old people, they don't feel that it is worth while and they won't stick. There is a certain class of trained nurses you can get, but they are worn out, and they are unable to do the ward work.   They are mighty glad to come and sit down in our institutions and direct this one or that one to do the work.   That one is a drone to your institution and the sooner you get rid of her the better.

There is a great need in this field for a nurse that has been trained in this kind of work. but in the general hospital they are so trained that they won't go into the ordinary Alms house, or go into some of our wards where there are insane inmates.

CHAIRMAN SCANLON: We have a trained nurse in our institution, and we also have two practical nurses. We won't stand for it for a minute where the nurse thinks she is merely an overseer, and our Board of Directors stand back of it.

MR. WILLIAM HILL: I can't sit still and hear you talk about the trained nurses because I married one. I listened to the gentleman from Blair County who said that he paid his trained nurse $80 per month. One of the previous speakers said that the good trained nurse is half doctor, and I will venture to say that the full-doctor wouldn't put in the time for three times $20 a week. Therefore you can't expect a woman who has taken up a profession to go into an institution and be on duty practically 24 hours a day for the same price that a girl who works in a store, or works in a factory, where they don't have to study for those positions. I think the greatest trouble is that you don't pay them enough.

I come from a district where we don't receive a salary. I understand that most of you men do, anywhere from $1,500 to $3,500 a year, and why should you expect a trained nurse to work for less than $1,000 a year. It is like buying a car. If you want a good automobile you don't buy a Ford, but you will pay the price and get a good car.

I am sure if you pay the money the trained nurses will stay. That is their work, they have specialized in that kind of work. They like it and they don't go flying about. They work and they like their work. We have reasons to know that is true from the experience of the last war. They did their work and they did it well.

MRS. E. C. DUNN: I have been a trained nurse for 27 years. I bless Mr. Hill for marrying a trained nurse, and I bless him for his kind words.

I agree with Mr. Hill regarding the salary, and I don't think we are paying our nurses enough.

I ask you, what is the attraction at our County Homes? I would like to know. As a rule all of our superintendents are married men. And not only that but most of their wives are matrons and what trained nurse is going to take up with the work there. I am not talking about the trained nurses of my day.

CHAIRMAN SCANLON: I might state that we pay our trained nurse $150 per month.

MRS. E. C. DUNN: Where do you come from?

CHAIRMAN SCANLON: We give her a month's vacation and one day a week off.

This summer I visited an institution where the man and his wife did most all of the work. His wife cooks for over 200 inmates, besides the help. I noticed the room where they kept the drugs, and I said to this man, "I see you are a druggist". I knew that he was not of course, and he told me that he handled the medicines. I asked him if he had a trained nurse, and he said that he didn't.

MRS. E. C. DUNN: I just want to say a few more words, if I may. When we talk about trained nurses we should not talk about the flapper type of trained nurse. Around good old mothers and fathers is no place for the foolish girl. We should have a sensible person, a trained woman who knows how to take care of the old people of our County.

You speak about the doctors. They are not in it with the nurses. The nurses are on duty practically 24 hours a day, and I take my hat off to the good old fashioned trained nurse.

MR. A. G. SEYFERT: They say that when the nurse is in the home she is a regular intolerant boss of that home while she is working there. If that be true, then that explains what Mr. White brought out a little while ago, that the trained nurse will not work with the superintendent of the home. Without discussing it any further than that, I just want to say this:

I have had some experience along that line, and I think there is more truth than fiction in it, because I have a daughter who is a trained nurse, and since she came from the army she wants to boss me and everybody else.

MRS. E. C. DUNN: How many nurses do you have at $150 per month?

CHAIRMAN SCANLON: We have just one, and she is in charge.

MRS. E. C. DUNN: How many patients do you have?

CHAIRMAN SCANLON: About 208 or 210.

MRS. E. C. DUNN: And you have attendants?

CHAIRMAN SCANLON: Yes. We call them wardens.

MRS. E. C. DUNN: Then she covers the entire institution?

CHAIRMAN SCANLON: Yes. We have two practical nurses, one on night duty and one on day duty. And then we have the day and night wardens.

MRS. T. C. WHITE: I would just like to add a little to what Mr. White has said. I have been at the institution for almost 10 years and during that time seven attendants have entered hospitals for training, the work having been so attractive to them.

We had an epidemic of the flu and we thought that we could handle it ourselves. Of course we were handicapped for room and we made our chapel into a regular hospital. During the day I practically took care of the patients, and Mr. White was on duty during the night, together with the assistance of some of the inmates.

Finally we were able to find a trained nurse who would come in and help us. She agreed to take care of the sick attendants, but would not nurse the patients who were insane.

We then got a trained nurse, and what did she do? She waited until I went in in the morning and had all of the beds changed and taken care of, the temperature taken, etc. Then she would take charge.

That has been our experience and that is why we feel as we do. We have not been able to find any one who would go in and do that hard work, even with the assistance of our patients.

The best thing we can do is to get good country girls with good common sense, and train them. We have had the most wonderful success in this respect. We have had very poor success with trained nurses.

CHAIRMAN SCANLON: I would like to ask Mr. Mackin to give us a few pointers with regard to his hospital.

MR. D. A. MACKIN: Our organization is worked out on the proposition of hospitalization of the County Home, or taking care of the chronically ill.

We all know that it is essential at this time, because regardless of how much good work is being done by the general hospital, it is physically impossible for them to take care of a patient that requires a week or month, or year to make any progress. It is unfair for the general hospital to take care of a convalescent patient who may remain for a long time.

To any one who is a student of the County Home, and realizes the changing conditions, it wouldn't take long to figure out that an institution of any size must change its methods if it is going to continue to exist, with the approval of the public. And the public is studying these questions today. Today we have the respect of the community, the State Welfare Department, and others. We are working out an organization as best we can.

We have a daily average of better than 400 patients. We have a resident physician in the home. Of course at Retreat we have the mental side, with three physicians there who may be called in for consultation if necessary.

Just recently a graduate nurse that was with me 25 years died. She gave her life to this kind of work. Perhaps I was a little pessimistic when I stated we could not hold them, but we did hold her for 25 years. I have one that has been with me for four years, and she is a graduate of a good New York hospital. She is willing to roll up her sleeves and go to work.

At Retreat we do not figure the hospital maintenance separately, but figure it as part of our institution. We figure that the average per patient is $6.12 per week, and I think it has reached as high as $6.74. I think it will run about $6 this year.

I hate to talk per capita cost. What do you get for your dollar! That is the point! We don't care for they are only relative figures. If you are satisfied that you are getting results commensurate with the money expended, that is what you want. There are too many people trying to work out a low per capita cost.

MR. CASPAR M. TITUS: I am very glad that Mr. Mackin spoke the way he did. What we are up against is this: We have, I would say, about 75 people at our institution who are inmates. When we have any real sick patients we send them to the Philadelphia hospital. At first they were willing to take them at $3.75, and then it began to go higher and higher. The charge now is $9.75, and within the next month it will possibly go twice $9.75.

I don't know if the laws are different in other localities or not, but Mrs. Megee told us when she visited our institution that in some places in order to operate a hospital ward you must have a day and night nurse, and also a resident physician. This would apply to the care of our 75 the same as the 400 at Retreat, and if this is the case then I don't think it would pay us to take care of only a few in this way.

I am glad that my Directors are present this afternoon and listen to this discussion. That will enlighten us wonderfully so that we can go back and feel free to discuss what we have heard here today.

MR. D. A. MACKIN: I would say that the small institution which is located near a general hospital, and that hospital will take care of those who are ill at the rate of $20 a week, are blessed.

The whole trouble is that we cannot apply this successfully to the very small institution. The cost is prohibitive. If you have between 150 or 200 patients who are chronically ill, then it is a different proposition.

I was asked to talk at the Sesqui-Centennial, and I read from manuscript for I did not want to be misquoted. I made the statement that 95 per cent of the patients upon medical examination were suffering from a definitely diagnosed disease. That was the result of my study in our own hospital covering a period of two years.

The speaker following me was a gentlemen from Massachusetts, and had been for 25 years in the work and had completed a survey of Massachusetts. He also read from manuscript, so we had not compared notes beforehand. And also we were not telling funny stories. He stated that from his survey 96 per cent of those admitted to all of the institutions were sick people who required medical attention. I don't mean that they need a doctor every day, but are suffering from chronic diseases, the most prevalent being heart disease.

MR. CASPAR M. TITUS: Mr. Chairman, I am awfully sorry to take up your time, but what I am going to say may assist somebody else.

We have four outside doctors, those whom we call our doctors on the outside. If some one is reported to our Board of Directors, then one of these doctors is called to attend that particular person, for the nominal sum of $200 per year. It is more of a charitable proposition than anything else. And then we have our visiting physician who receives $300 per year and he calls as often as it is necessary.

I again want to urge that my Directors get as much of this information as they can so that they will know how to vote when this proposition comes up again.

The people on the outside state we should maintain a hospital and we on the inside figure that it wouldn't be a paying proposition to employ the required number of nurses and doctors where you only have 75 people in the institution.

I am very much interested in this discussion.

Mr. Charles L. Huston: Mr. Chairman, we have had a superintendent at the Chester County Home for 25 years and finally he broke down in health. He resigned and we didn't know where we were going to get a man with the qualifications.

The man we did get we secured from the railroad station. Some folks said, "What experience has that man had to run a County Home?" We found that we had the ideal man.

While this man was at the railroad station he had time to look after other business. While he had charge of the railroad station he had some experience in handling freight, thereby giving him the strength in which to handle particular cases at the County Home.

He secured his business experience during the time he was connected with the railroad.

He had farm experience, for he conducted a farm on the side during the time he had charge of the railroad station, and he accumulated enough money upon which to live comfortably and have something to spare.

I wish to state that he has brought that institution up in every way. The place is kept clean and the people are kept clean. The business management has gone on without any increase in the budget, with the exception of when the prices increase.

The man to whom I refer is Mr. W. B. Passmore, and I would like to have him make a few remarks at this time.

Mr. W. B. Passmore: That was quite an introduction, I am sure.

I have been a very busy man all my life. I brought the Directors of the Poor up here yesterday on my way to Reading, and on the way I stopped to pay a little visit. I told the Directors that I wanted to pay a little visit at the house. I got out, and then introduced my mother to them. I said to them, "I have been keeping my mother ever since I was 14 years of age and I have never lost anything by doing it."

I want to speak to you regarding the engaging of trained nurses. One man stated that he paid $80 a month, and another one stated that he paid as high as $150 a month. and also a man in the back of the room stated that he had married one. My daughter was a trained nurse and after she had been in that work for a year she married the man she was nursing.

In Chester County we employ a trained nurse to take care of our sick people. We pay her $120 per month, and I find there is no better way in which to conduct an institution than to engage a trained nurse.

Six months ago our practical nurse in the County Home part seemed to get more or less dissatisfied. She was a very good practical nurse, and it seemed that her nerves broke down. She took a rest. At that time I said, "I am going to make a change and put in her place a trained nurse in the wards of the County Home.

I might state that we have 185 people in the County Home wards and 348 or 350 in the insane department.

I engaged two trained nurses and had them I think about two months, and what happened? They wanted off every Saturday afternoon, part day Sunday, and it got so that they were absolutely no good to me at all. I went back and got the old practical nurse. I had been paying her $80 per month, and when she came back I increased her salary to $100 per month.

I want to say to you men and women who are located at a County Home, when you get hold of a good practical nurse, and pay her $125 a month, you have somebody that is going to do you some good.

However, when you come down to the other case, such as the contageous cases or the cases which take a little more skill, you must have a trained nurse.

After all you must work out your own problems in the particular community in which you are located, for you know what is best for the County Home there. I thank you.

CHAIRMAN SCANLON: We will now go on to the subject, "**Diet in the County Home,**" which will be presented by **Miss Madge T. Bogart,** in charge of the Home Economics Extension Service, Pennsylvania State College. I take pleasure in introducing at this time Miss Bogart.

FOOD IN ITS RELATION TO THE DAILY MENU
Miss Madge T. Bogart

It has been said that food, in sustaining a race of people in good health and vigor, performs four functions These functions are the operation, growth, repair and reproduction of the body substance. The human body contains many chemical elements in varying amounts. Nitrogen, carbon, hydrogen and oxygen are the four present in largest proportion. Iron, phosphorous, calcium, magnesium, potassium, sodium, sulphur, chlorin, iodin, also have important offices to perform. Foods must contain the same elements found in the body so that the food may perform the four functions mentioned.

The foods which perform these four functions are generally classified under the following headings:

I. Fuel Foods—Carbohydrates.

II. Body Building Foods—Proteins and Calcium, Phosphorous and Iron.

III. Body Regulating and Protective Foods.

I. Fuel Foods or carbohydrates are those which yield energy.

a. Sugars

Source—juices of sweet fruits and vegetables, oranges, grapes, apples, corn, peas, etc.

b. Starches

Source—wheat, oats, corn and other grains, potatoes, tapioca, bananas, nuts, peas, beans, etc.

c. Fats

Cream, butter, animal fats, olives, cottonseed, peanuts, cocoa beans, etc.

II. Body building foods—Protein, Calcium, Phosphorous, Iron, (build and repair tissues, muscles, bone, blood and nerves).

a. Protein (build and repair tissues)

Sources—Milk, cheese, eggs, meat, fish, legumes (peas beans) nuts and cereals.

b. Calcium (essential for strong bones and teeth)

Sources—Milk, cheese, eggs, vegetables, whole grains.

c. Phosphorous (forms part of every active cell and helps with calcium to give rigidity to bones and teeth).

Sources—Milk, cheese, egg yolk, whole grains, fruits and vege- tables.

d. Iron—(in red corpuscles of blood, essential to conveyance of oxygen to the cells and hence to the burning of fuel foods and is an ele- ment in the structure of all active cells).

Sources—Egg yolk, green vegetables especially spinach and fruits.

III. Body regulating and Protective Foods.

1. Mineral or Ash Constituents (help blood maintain its neutrality, the heart its regular beat, nerves and muscles respond readily to every impulse.)

Source—Milk, eggs, dried peas, beans, fresh fruits, vegetables, and whole grains.

2. Water—(regulates body temperature. Helps regulate concentration of mineral elements, helps in transportation of materials to tis- sues by holding them in solution in body fluids, and helps in removal of waste).

3. Vitamins—(Vitamins seem, in a way, to be natures' drugs, stimulating the body cells in order that they may function in a normal man- ner, absolutely essential to promote growth and maintain health and well-being).

1. Vitamin A. (fat soluble necessary for growth and prevention of eye disease xerphthalmia).

Source—Milk, butter, cod-liver oil, egg yolk, and green leafy vegetables.

2. Vitamin B (water soluble—stimulates the appetite and helps the body to become strong and resistant to disease and ex- posure).

Source—yeast, cereals, vegetables, fruits, small quantities in milk and eggs.

3. Vitamin C (prevents development of scurvy)
Source—Tomatoes, oranges, lemons and· all citrus fruits, raw
   cabbage, also in cows milk if the cow has been fed a vitamin rich
   ration
4. Vitamin D (fat soluble—prevents rickets).
Source—Cod-liver oil, ultra-violet light produced by the quartz
   mercury vapor lamp, fresh alfalfa, egg yolk.
5. Vitamin E—(reproduction vitamin)
Source—oats, corn and wheat (whole cereal) lettuce, lean meat.

IV. Cellulose or Roughage—(helps in regulating body processes)
   Source—Whole grain products—bran, fruits with skin and green
      vegetables.

In addition to this classification of foods is another one of comparatively
recent discovery and exceedingly important. It is now known and recognized that our diet must contain the proper proportion and ratio of foods
that produce two opposite results when finally digested and ready for
absorption by the cells. One of these end-products is called Alkalin and
the other Acid. The correct proportion and ratio between these two is
about 80 to 20. That is, the blood and cells of the body should exhibit a
ratio of 80 units Alkalin elements to 20 units of Acid elements.

Just so long as about the correct proportion between these is established
and maintained, our bodies are properly nourished and the system is able
to defend itself against diseases and the activities of the body are prolonged.

The Alkalin-forming foods are known to be the non-starchy vegetables.
All fruits (except large prunes, plums, cranberries, and half-ripe bananas),
salad greens, lettuce, celery, parsley. etc.

The Acid-forming foods are all proteins, beef, mutton, pork, veal, fish,
fowl, game, sea-foods, cheese, bread, cake, pastry (anything made from
any kind of grain), potatoes, rice, dry beans and peas, sugar, salt, half-ripe
bananas, large prunes, plums, cranberries, rhubarb, nuts, etc.

Nutritional investigations have shown us that all the components of
food do not perform the functions equally well. That each component
performs special functions of its own. Hence in order to have a so-called
"balanced diet" we must select foods which will provide fuel for all body
activities and these must be accompanied by or include those substances
which serve to build up the organism. These foods must be· in the right
proportion and ratio to keep the Alkalin and Acid content of the blood and
cells about normal so as to keep them functioning properly.

In other words this means that our diet should include :

6-8 glasses of water a day.
1 quart of milk for each child.
1 pint of milk for each adult.

Two vegetables a day other than potatoes—such as carrots, string beans,
beets, peas, corn, asparagus, lima beans, onions, etc.

Greens twice a week—such· as spinach, kale, swiss chard, beet tops, New
Zealand spinach, wild greens, endive, etc.

Tomatoes twice a week.

A raw vegetable twice a week—such as cabbage, lettuce, raw carrots, celery, endive, dandelion, chinese cabbage, etc.

Two fruits a day—one preferably fresh, the other canned or dried.

Eat meat not more than once a day. Get the protein supply also from milk, eggs, cheese, bread, nuts, etc.

Such a diet will promote growth, health and well being. It is not necessary to have elaborate cookery or many kinds of food but rather a simple menu carefully chosen and the food carefully prepared. Warm food usually adds to the case with which a meal is digested and often to its relish.

The diet we have already discussed applies especially to the normal individual. Up to the age of sixty reductions in food are necessitated chiefly by lessened external muscular activity and excess of food is stored as body fat. In really old people there is a decided retardation of the internal processes and caring for excess food becomes more difficult. There is a tendency to lose rather than to gain body weight. The dangers of excess are greater than dangers of under-nutrition. Hence serve a well balanced diet but serve smaller portions. As long as there is life there will be some exchange of materials in the process of cell activity and none of the elements already seen to be essential to a well-balanced dietary can be entirely dispensed with. It is just that the total amount required is less than ever before.

One of the difficulties of old age is loss of the power of mastication. When the teeth become useless, digestion will be interfered with if foods aren't provided which do not require chewing. We can get the protein requirement from milk, soft cooked eggs, easily flaked fish and finely scraped or minced meats. If the gums cannot masticate breadstuffs the result is likely to be fermentation. Then substitute very crisp toast or zwieback, softened in milk, tea, coffee, soup, etc. This change in texture makes the food break up readily into small pieces and it will digest more rapidly. Use thoroughly cooked cereals and baked potatoes. Sugars are valuable if they can be taken without fermentation. Many old people are fond of sweets and can eat considerable amounts without indigestion.

Fats should be used sparingly on account of the slowing of digestive processes and slowing of the flowing of the digestive juices. Discard the use of rich sauces, cakes, puddings, pastries, and fried foods. Forms of fats which can be easily used are cream, butter, bacon and olive oil. Use these with bread, cereals, etc.

Warm foods is desirable to stimulate gastric secretion and aid digestion especially in the aged. Use a warm beverage such as tea or coffee or a clear soup instead of a glass of cold water at the beginning of a meal.

How freely fruits and green vegetables may be used depends much upon the individual. They may make up a considerable part of the dietary if mastication is possible and fermentation does not develop. If this is the case vegetables and fruits must be given in the same ways as they would be given to children. Fruits as juice or stewed pulp of mild varieties; vegetables well cooked and mashed or put through a sieve and served as puree or soup. In many ways the diet for old people is similar to that fed to children in the first five or six years—fruit juices, well cooked cereals, milk, eggs, strained vegetables and cereal puddings. The emphasis on building materials is less and hot and stimulating foods such as tea and coffee are added to the aged persons menu.

Many old people sleep better with some form of nourishment when they go to bed or when they waken in the night. Hot milk, cereal gruel, hot malted milk, hot bouillon or warm water. Sometimes when an old person wakes early in the morning they desire food before the regular breakfast hour. They might have a few plain crackers, fruit juice or a glass of milk. These additions to the regular menu may increase the number of meals in extreme old age to five or six a day.

In closing I want to emphasize the fact that in the diets of old people the keynote to health is moderation and simplicity in a well balanced diet.

CHAIRMAN SCANLON: The next will be the third subject, "The Tramp and Vagrant Problem." I will call upon Dr. W. L. Henderson, Director, Allegheny County. (Not present)

I will call upon Miss Esther Martin, Investigator, Beaver County.

MISS ESTHER MARTIN: Mr. Chairman, Ladies and Gentlemen: In considering the first, the common tramp which you are accustomed to meeting in your own communities, fortunately that problem is not a great one for us at the Beaver County Home. We are not located on a direct highway, and our County Home is situated on the southern bank of the Ohio River. Consequently we are not bothered much with the common tramp.

I don't think we have more than a dozen vagrants a year, and the reason for it is because we are off the beaten track. This problem is well taken care of by the jails and is the problem of various boroughs. We have 26 boroughs in the county that follow the river, and I know that some of those jails have from 25 to 40 on a cold morning. This matter has been handled very well by the boroughs. I suppose that if the County Home were available, or there was street car service to it, we might get them. We do have a few old men who come in and stay over the week-end, and then go on their way.

I happen to be the welfare worker for the commissioners, and we make an investigation of every case that goes to the County Home. If it is possible to maintain an individual in his own home, or the home of some one who will keep him at small expense, we let him stay there. Of course if the maintenance becomes greater than what it would be at the County Home, he is taken there.

With regard to the vagrant problem, if we have some men there who are able-bodied men able to work, and who are not inclined to do any work, they usually don't stay long. Our women of course wouldn't come under that heading.

The other type of vagrant is the deserter. I think Beaver County has its proportion, but we have the cooperation of the judges and in any case where a family comes to us on the grounds of desertion and non-support, we insist upon information relative to the location of the man, unless it is an unusual situation. Every bit of information is obtained and we don't take the family's word for it. There are cases where the man got out and by the time the family would receive assistance then he would return.

As I said, an investigation is made. The commissioners of Beaver County (who also act as Poor Directors) believe that it is much cheaper to bring a man back to support the family than to maintain the family, and every method is made to apprehend him and bring him back.

The first time, the man is under court order and is placed under bond. He is made to work and support his family. The second or third offenses are treated that way, and the fourth time he is sent to the workhouse.

I know that some of the neighboring counties think that it is too expensive to bring the man back, but I might state that we have brought them back from Illinois and various other places. The costs are attached to the man's court costs and in this way he must pay them back.

This type of vagrant, of course, is dealt with through the courts, and I just thought I would mention it for the benefit of those present.

CHAIRMAN SCANLON: Is there any discussion on this subject?

MR. R. C. BUCHANAN: I would like to ask Miss Martin how she handles the bootlegger.

MISS ESTHER MARTIN: The bootlegging case is rather difficult to handle. It takes three or four times as much investigation because usually they have money somewhere. If we find that they have, and the man is sent to the workhouse, we try to keep the family together.

MR. R. C. BUCHANAN: In our county usually when the man is sent up for bootlegging, the wife will follow him, and then we must take care of the children.

MISS ESTHER MARTIN: That is a problem which everybody is working with. We do get them and we have had them.

I know of one case not long ago. The judge asked me to make an investigation, and upon investigation we found that they had $10,000 that they were not telling anybody about. It wasn't banked, and by going back through the routine of the arrest, and talking with the person who made the original arrest, it was learned that this woman had a large roll of bills which she accused this man of taking.

We must be very careful. We must use judgment in securing this information, and we do not try to get information from the bank until the last resort. It sometimes takes a real detective to handle the cases, but we have no particular solution for it.

CHAIRMAN SCANLON: We will now hear from Mr. T. Springer Todd, of Fayette County.

MR. T. SPRINGER TODD: Mr. Chairman, Ladies and Gentlemen: I don't know that I have anything in particular to say pertaining to the running of an institution.   I have been superintendent of the Fayette County Home 'or about 9 years, and of course we are learning something new every day and every day

I really don't think that there are any two institutions which are operated just exactly alike in the State   I have my way of running the Fayette County Home, and you have your way, but I think the biggest factor in the successful operation of any home is the cooperation of your Board of Directors.

There are no two minds which run alike, and the biggest thing is to have the Board of Directors and the superintendent cooperate with each other. Without that, Mr. Chairman, I can't see where any superintendent can make a success in the operation of a home.

There are so many more people here who have had so much more experience than I have, and I would like to have their views on it.

I am for the Board and all that, but at the same time the Board has absolutely got to be with the superintendent.

I thank you.

CHAIRMAN SCANLON: I would like to have Mr. William H. F. Kuhns speak to us at this time.   (Not present)

I will ask Mr. Horn, of Montgomery County to say a few words to us.

MR. MARTIN L. HORN: Mr. Chairman, I am not on the program, so I am not in position to talk on the subject at the present time, thank you.

CHAIRMAN SCANLON: Mr. Mackin, could you tell us something about the subject, "Administration of County Homes?"

MR. D. A. MACKIN: I have answered so many questions relative to the conducting of our County Home that I don't know what I would add.

I presume we operate our home the same as most of the institutions are operated; that is, admission to the County Home is by order of the Director.   We assume ordinarily that investigation has been made.   However, very often we have made discoveries after the patient has come to us that the relatives of the patient have the ability to assist financially toward the support of the patient.

With regard to the financial problems, we do, of course, operate a central office in the city of Wilkes-Barre and all financial problems are handled there.   The secretary, who is also a member of the Board, is on duty continuously.

Our Directors employ three investigators who are continuously at work, doing principally outdoor work.   Very often, in the course of their activities, they steer cases away from the institution, being able to place them in another way.

When a patient is brought to us, a physical examination is made within 24 hours after arrival. Under normal conditions the patient is examined within two or three hours after coming to us. Their case is recorded immediately after diagnosing the case. The patient is then placed in the institution according to the physical condition, classifications having been made.

Most people have an idea that when people are sent to the County Home they are all mixed up in one great group. This is not true in most of the County Homes. If you have buildings enough and your institution is large enough, then you can classify them. We classify all patients as to their physical condition. We also classify them as to their language.

In this locality there are between 40 and 50 per cent foreign population, the non-English speaking people. We rarely place an English speaking person in with the foreigner.

Miner's asthma was mentioned, and I presume that most of you are not familiar with miner's asthma. It would be impossible to place one afflicted with miner's asthma in the same room with a rheumatic patient. The one afflicted with miner's asthma must have the windows wide open, and the rheumatic patient must be kept warm.

If we don't handle the cases properly then we will be subject to criticism. I think that is about all I have to say, Mr. Chairman.

CHAIRMAN SCANLON: The next subject is, "Has the County Home Outlived its Usefulness?" The first speaker is Mr. Lorrie R. Holcomb, Esq., of the Central Poor District of Luzerne County. Is Mr. Holcom present? (Not present.)

MR. D. A. MACKIN: I might state that the subject was suggested to me by reason of the criticism of certain articles which have appeared in magazines and in the New York papers. written very largely by the Secretary of Labor, Mr. Davis.

I am not going to criticise the Secretary of Labor, because a whole lot of what he said is true, but my point is that the whole thing is generalized.

Most of the County Homes are good County Homes, and we are suffering because of the few poor ones in this state and the poor ones throughout the country, particularly the ones in the southern part of the country.

MISS ESTHER MARTIN: I would just like to say a few words about this. We have a tuberculosis hospital, and one of the best county jails in the state because it is watched very carefully by the commissioners. And of course we have our County Home, and most of the people have the impression that we dump the people into this home and then go away and leave them.

I started out to do outdoor relief work only, and it wasn't long before they asked me to take this other work over. Our population hasn't increased since I have been in that work, but we have taken in a number of cases who were past the danger stage.

We don't have a hospital there. That thing has been under consideration a number of times.

During the winter we will have as high as 100, but it usually runs around 85. A number of our patients have been taken care of by the local hospital. Our commissioners think that it is too expensive to operate our hospital ward, and those who need attention are taken to the hospital. The State Department doesn't like it so well, and the hospitals are not keen about doing that, but it isn't possible to take care of them in any other way. We have our own tuberculosis hospital and the tuberculosis patients are taken care of in that way.

From the experience I have had, and the knowledge working with this problem, I would say that the County Home has not outlived its usefulness.

The commissioners had that very thing up for discussion not long ago, and it was discovered taking into consideration the character of the cases, you couldn't get anybody else to take care of them. There will always be cases of like nature, and I believe these previous speakers are right for we know ourselves that a great proportion of our inmates are mentally and physically ill.

I have been in the work four years and since I first came in there has been a big change, and I think you all recognize that. I think the County Home has not outlived its usefulness, but their general use is being changed in another direction.

MR. D. GLENN MOORE: I have had an intimate relation with the Washington County Home for the past 10 years, and when Mr. Mackin referred to Secretary Davis' articles, I must say that I don't have a very high regard for Mr. Davis' knowledge of social problems at all. Some parts of the articles are true no doubt, but the greater bulk of them are untrue as far as the average home is concerned. There are some Homes which cannot be compared with the average home.

If we were to take away the County Homes this week, we would have to open them up again next week. There is no alternative for the County Home. If there are bad County Homes it is on account of the humanity in the immediate community.

I will put up our County Home against any institution, public, semi-public or private. I know all of the patients in our home intimately, and some of them I have known since boyhood. Some of them are living better today than they ever did in their lives, or their parents before them.

It is not such a big problem as Mr. Davis would try to bring out. We have about 237 there, and they all have a clean place in which to live and they have good wholesome food to eat.

Before I finish I just want to mention the Old Age Pension. They tell us that we should have an Old Age Pension, and I am here to say that they will spend their dollar and will be in the County Home anyway.

REV. P. L. CARPENTER: I was waiting for some one to say something about the Old Age Pension. For nearly 18 years I have been making the County Home and County Prison the study of my life. . I might shock this crowd this afternoon if I were to say what has been in my mind. And I am going to say it, not because I am fixed, but I wonder after all in the final outcome, whether that wouldn't be the best thing.

· I think that every Poor House, (I don't care what the name you address it under) is a Poor House regardless whether you call it a County Home or not.

I am open to criticism, but from a deep conviction I think that it is practically disgraceful to every community. What do I mean? We hear oftentimes of the unfortunate poor. They are so few. But the vast number of careless poor.

I have been wondering whether the time ever might come when your own poor in your own community might be boarded out to some home, other than an institutional home. The County Home is an institution, not a home. I have an object in that thought.

You have your sick among the poor. You must have your County Hospital. And then there is the Insane Hospital and the Alms House.

Somehow or other I am forced to believe that some people look forward to that day when they get tired of the struggle of life, that they may go to the Poor House.

I say this, that when old people cannot take care of themselves, they should be taken care of by the county. And as Miss Martin has said, make a thorough investigation.

However, I am forced to believe that conditions are not getting better, and they will continue to get worse if something isn't done. I wish we could study that question, but as I say after 18 years of a deep earnest study of the work, I am almost forced to believe that if possible we should keep our old people together, man and wife, and pay somebody who might look after them, saving them the disgrace of going into a County Poor house.

Mrs. E. C. Dunn: How many homes do you have that would take them?

Rev. P. L. Carpenter: As I say, it would have to be worked out.

Mrs. E. C. Dunn: . I read the articles by Secretary Davis, and I would like to pull his hair if he has any. We have a home and we work well together, and to tell me that we can do without a home it will take an older man than Secretary Davis to tell me that.

Mr. A. G. Seyfert: The subject is "Has the County Home Outlived its Usefulness?" I emphatically say "no!"

And with regard to the Old Age Pension, I must say that I don't believe in socialistic ideas of any sort. The pensioning of paupers and vagrants along that line is nothing more than a socialistic idea, and the American people don't believe in it.. . The more pensions the more paupers.

If you were to give them $1 a day, as these people say, which would amount to $30 a month, or $365 per year, (and they cost that much perhaps in many of our Poor Houses, I will admit) at the end of the year they have no home, their money is gone, and they have nothing. The great majority of those people were never able to care for themselves, no matter how much they received. If you were to give them $5 a day and send them away from the home, then somebody would have to take care of them. Most of them are not normal, in their citizenship and conduct.

I absolutely have no use for a pension. It would not decrease the population in any of our Alms Houses.

Mention was made here to board them out. You all know about the history of that, when in England they boarded them out to the man who would bid the lowest. One fellow said he would keep them for $1.50 and another fellow would offer to keep them for $1, or less. The fellow who bid the lowest always got them. If you pension them and put them out of the Poor House, we will get back again virtually to where we started 400 years ago in England.

More than that, this pensioning business seems to be on the minds of a great many people—so that we can all live without doing anything. I am thoroughly opposed to the pension systems.

CHAIRMAN SCANLON: We would like to hear from Mr. R. C. Buchanan, Director, Washington County.

MR. R. C. BUCHANAN: I don't think I can add anything to what has already been said. Mr. Seyfert's views are my views to the letter.

To do away with the County Homes, and pension the old people, you would be boarding them out to the cheapest bidder, as Mr. Seyfert has said. The result would be that we would come down to the way we used to run the County Homes, feeding them on bread and molasses. That day has gone by. In our County Home they are better taken care of than they ever were in their own homes. We have quite a number at our home where their own people wouldn't take care of them, but they will pay us the sum of $20 a month to take care of the old father and mother. They are not satisfied to take care of their own people.

At the present time we have in our home over 90 inmates who are over 70 years of age. There is nobody to care for them. If you pension those old people, who is going to care for those old people over 70 years old?

Along the line of pensions, or compensation, which is practically the same thing, I was called upon to look into a certain case. There was a man at a hospital in Pittsburgh and they wanted to remove him to the County Home. I went to Pittsburgh and discovered that this man was getting compensation and wouldn't pay the hospital and wouldn't pay the County Home. He was sending his compensation check away to his sister in New Jersey.

Our solicitor, Mr. Jones, took it up with the compensation board and had that compensation twisted around so that this man would reimburse the County Home and hospital.

I am heartily in favor of what Mr. Seyfert has said, and I don't believe there is anything better than the County Homes at the present time.

MR. A. G. SEYFERT: I know that in Lancaster County at the Lancaster County Home there were some people pensioned by the United States Government, and received $50 per month. They couldn't live themselves on it, and how do you suppose they could live on $30 a month?

I merely mention that fact.

MR. CHARLES L. HUSTON: I think we have all had experience in this fact that the odium of sending the old folks to the County Home acts as a healthy stimulus to take care of them rather than to send them there. I don't want to make a bad thing for a good purpose, but if they were pensioned so that a lot of these people who want to get out from under their proper burden of taking care of the old people, and could have somebody else take care of them for pay, they would do less than they do now. It seems what we want to do is to bear down on the sons and daughters of the younger generation to make them take care of the older people and not ease up on that responsibility.

MR. D. A. MACKIN: The matter of the Old Age Pension is viewed entirely without sentiment, and its effect on the County Home.

On the first of January, 1926, I went into the question of my population at that time, at the request of Mr. Solenberger. Some Senator raised the question with him, and Mr. Solenberger raised the question with me. I went very carefully through that from the standpoint of determining how many of the inmates could be removed from the institution, gathering the data from a scientific standpoint, and I found that they couldn't move more than 10 per cent of our population, and I question if it would be 5 per cent.

CHAIRMAN SCANLON: Is there any further discussion? If not the meeting will stand adjourned until eight o'clock this evening.

... The meeting adjourned at 4:50 o'clock ...

TUESDAY EVENING·SESSION
October 4,·1927

The meeting convened at 8:15 o'clock, President Charles F. Loesel presiding.

PRESIDENT LOESEL: It is time for the convention to come to order. The invocation will be made by Rev. P. L Carpenter in absence of Rev. James A. Boland.

... Rev. Carpenter made the invocation at this time ...

PRESIDENT LOESEL: It gives me great pleasure at this time to introduce to you Mrs. Cornelia B. Meytrott, of the State Department Institutions and Agencies, Trenton, New Jersey.

STATE SUPERVISION

MRS. CORNELIA B. MEYTROTT: I am very happy to be here, and it was a pleasure to ride through your beautiful country. It is a privilege to be on your program, and tomorrow you have a program full of interesting things, and I refer to children's work.

I am sorry indeed that our commissioner himself could not come and talk to you, as Mr. Solenberger requested. I would like you to know what manner of man we have, and you would truly understand the good work of which I may tell you about this evening. Surely you didn't expect me to come and tell you about the bad work we might do and let other people do.

. Our own governor last week at a County Conference told us this story for the benefit of the representatives:

The young lady at confessional said, "I fear that I am falling into the the sin of vanity."

"Vanity," said the priest, "and why do you think you are falling into the sin of vanity?"

She replied, "Whenever I look into the mirror I say to myself, "How beautiful you are."

And the priest said, "That is not a sin, that is a mistake."

The governor had been listening to an eulogy about himself and he felt a bit modest.

New Jersey is a compact little State, and I am going to tell you one or two things about it, although you are next door neighbors, I take it for granted that you are not very familiar with it. ·

We are quite populous; I would say, with about two-thirds of our population centered in what we call the metropolitan area where New York, Patterson, Jersey City, and other cities practically merge.

But that isn't all, you know. We have that great shore city, Atlantic City, and also Asbury Park, Camden, and other cities of importance.

Our smaller political units we call boroughs, those which are not large enough to claim the title of city. And then we have a great number of townships which have separate or political units.

Whether it be a large city of a million inhabitants, or a small borough or rural township where they may have only 700 or 800 souls, in each of these we have an official which is termed an Overseer of the Poor. Here I believe they call them Directors of the Poor. No doubt they have larger territories and must have larger sounding names.

Our population totals 3,200,000 persons. Of these 27 per cent, plus, are foreign, or negro. Is that a surprise to you? Nearly one-third of the population (and I am basing these figures on the census of 1920) is foreign, and since then I am sure that the foreign population has increased.

According to the most recent federal study of Alms Houses and institutions which might be called Poor Homes, there were about 2,200 persons receiving care in these tax-supported institutions. In Pennsylvania the chances are one to a thousand that one will get to the Poor House, while in New Jersey the chances are not quite so great. We have a better chance of staying out. Ohio, with its population twice as great as that of New Jersey, has four times as many in its Poor Houses. Massachusetts has also a higher percentage and spends three times as much money per citizen.

However, many are cared for in our State institutions for the insane, for the tubercular, or in county hospitals for these two groups. Others, having some means, are in the 150 or more private nursing homes and Homes for the Aged.

Relief, in our State, is left in the hands of local officials, hence those clients not sent to hospitals for specialized treatment are not known to the State Department, but are provided for through the offiee of the Overseer of the Poor in each district, or by private social agencies.

Somebody made a mistake about our County Homes a year or so ago. A man from the West, who had a theory, published a book reporting what he termed a survey of Alms Houses in various states. And some of the things in that book were not very nice.

Mr Evans, the writer in question, did not survey our homes. He did not go into them. But he took some old records and culled from them what suited his purpose. He even went so far as to disregard punctuation and context, stopping in the middle of a sentence or phrase so the words would fit in the pattern he was setting up.

Just to give you an example, he stated in his book, "The State Board of Control for four years ending 1922, referring to the Poor Farms says, "They are in a sad state."

In that report of the State Board of Control it says: "Generally the Alms Houses were, with notable exceptions, in a sad state before and during the war, but through cooperation general extensive improvements have been made."

If you have read things that don't sound nice about conditions in some of the Alms Houses, I hope you will remember that the study of our institutions were made from ancient records, and that only parts were taken from them so as to make it fit into what was desired.

In February of this year, I visited many of these institutions in company with agents of the National Civic Federation. Near Jersey City is the Hudson county group, including a home proper, and two hospitals, one for tubercular cases and the other for the chronically ill. No general hospital anywhere is more perfectly equipped or ably staffed for the task of relieving suffering, and restoring strength.

Near Camden is another colony, a two million dollar plant with separate units for these respective groups of aged and dependent persons.

Trenton Municipal Colony adds to these a special building for the segregation of venereal cases.

Away down in Cape May county a very rural, sparsely settled community, they have an ideal home, and with it a hospital unit.

The usual exception to the rule in public institutions we found in Perth Amboy. On the whole, however, it was surprising how clean, well furnished and well managed they were. And I think you will find that in the report of the National Civic Federation.

The need for more complete segregation of the sick, and for more nursing and medical care in the smaller counties and cities is the most outstanding criticism. But, what authority has the State Department over these homes?

To the welfare division of the Department of Institutions and Agencies, is delegated the duty of inspection of these, and by an act of the last legislature, the inspection and licensing of all private nursing or boarding homes also.

No State official or department has summary powers. As I explained before, New Jersey is committed to home rule. However, there are two ways to get at an unsatisfactory situation, namely, the gentle way, through the Board of Freeholders, and as a last recourse, the grand jury indictment.

The Board of Freeholders is the governing body of the county. With individual boards and with their State Association, our department is always in close cooperative relations; we are inter-dependent in so many welfare problems.

You see now what is our avenue of approach to County Homes, and the gate is wide open. In regards to the city institutions, it is the same, with the exception that we work with the City Commission.

At the present time it appears that persons admitted to care in tax-supported homes, are much more likely to receive proper care and treatment. The latter, unless fortunate enough to get into a well established home, are likely to become the victims of the commercialized boarding home. In some of these, I have seen conditions which beggar description.

That is where our principal attack will be directed during the year to come. The last Legislature gave us the authority, and when I tell you that Dr. Potter is organizing this work among other large jobs she has undertaken for us, you know how wisely, kindly and effectively it will be done.

We believe in the Lord, and the Prophets. New decalogues are popular, so I have devised one for Overseers, or Directors of the Poor, as you know them better:

1. "Thou shalt have no political gods; to bow down or worship them."

2. "Six days shalt thou labor, but it shall not be all thy work, for many do 'fall into the pit' on the Sabbath."

3. "Honor thy public, that thy days may be long in the post wherein they have put thee."

4. "Thou shalt not fail to hearken to the widow, and the orphan."

5. "Thou shalt not waste."

6. "Thou shalt not listen to false witness, but know it for what it is."

7. "The deserting father shalt thou find, and visit his sins upon him."

8. "Thou shalt love every one's neighbor as thyself, lest any be found wanting."

The rest, dear people, I leave to you!

When we passed the new revision of the Poor Laws there was quite a struggle with the Overseers; they thought it would rob them of their glory. On the contrary, it has exalted the office. Their real quarrel with the law now, is that there is so much of it—72 pages long—and the first requirement of an Overseer is that he must "know his law.'

These men and women are appointed for five-year terms by the governing body of the municipality. Salaries are fixed by the appointing body. To be eligible, one must be a citizen, literate, have a knowledge of the Poor Law, and be of good character. The appointing power may require Civil Service examinations. The Overseer has power to make decisions, and authority to enforce them. He may appoint his own deputies and volunteers. He is not limited in expenditure for necessary relief to a fixed amount appropriated but shall grant relief in his discretion. It is possible, you see, to make this office one of commanding interest and importance.

Under the permissive act, poor districts may combine into a larger unit and employ a full-time Overseer. If he serves an entire county, he shall be known as the County Superintendent of Welfare, and shall be the chief executive of the County Welfare House.

We are back to where we began, back to the County Home, which, with a new name, has also under the provisions of this law, a somewhat different character. It is intended that the Welfare House shall be so organized and maintained as to overcome many of the old objections to the "Poor House." That it shall be in part a home, part a hospital, or in other words, a place to which aged persons, whether well or ill, if they have no home of their own, will feel they can come. Or, to describe in the words of one of its advocates, "It is to be the sort of institution which will be a comfort to you, when you go to see it, where the old people may find dignity, happiness and peace." And don't build it until you are ready to build it in that way.

So much for the law. How are these things going to happen? I said we believe in the Prophets. It takes a good deal of prophesying to accomplish social progress. I mean, not so much foretelling, warning, but leading and teaching the people to actually think on social questions, and try to find the answer. It is, in reality, educating people up to the point where they are ready to take a forward step. It takes time, we admit, and you must wait for them to grow up with the thought. You won't find it worth while in the end to just change their minds for them.

On Tuesday of last week I saw some of the fruits of this kind, and as it concerned one subject, I will just describe the scene for you.

It was a perfect, sunny afternoon. For more than an hour cars rolled into the drive at Brookdale, the country estate of the president of the County Organization for Social Service. Scores of cars, official and unofficial, luxurious limousines and humble "rattle boxes," from every corner of the county and beyond.

In a brief time, five hundred chairs set under the trees, and more in the spacious porch, were all occupied. Differences in rank, in politics, in faith in wealth and social distinction—all were forgotten. A Republican leader of the Senate introduced our Democratic Governor, Edward Moore, with a eulogy. Nurses in uniform were alternated on the program with state officials, and Overseers of the Poor, Freeholders, and Home Managers followed physician and clergymen—all were thinking and talking about the same subject, it being the establishment of a Welfare House in Monmouth County. And that is what the meeting accomplished. The Freeholders, who spend the people's money, know now that they, the people, want it spent in that way, that they need it. Not one has any longer any doubt, and they want that kind of care for their aged.

Do you think this Welfare House was built in a day? It was not. The meeting I have described is the fruit of patient planting and nurturing of the idea in the public mind.

I think in New Jersey we have demonstrated this principle many times. What we have today is sound organization or effective discharge of public responsibility has come in response to demand, the result of educated public opinion. As a result we feel that our institutional work is on a firm basis. We enjoy fairly generous support of our program for relief, reform and correction. Coupled with support of the State program, and linking together of State, County and community, there is an increasing appreciation of the importance of the private agency, and the inter-dependence of all.

.The work of all State institutions is, as you know, coordinated very actively under the State Board of Control, acting through the Commission-er and his central staff. The State program is interlocked with county work at many points, and both in turn find many important points of contact with local and private agencies.

I think to sum it up, we do our best to meet the needs of the aged, as other social needs in manner which will do us credit. We believe that progress toward this goal is, by a process of growing rather than forcibly changing or adding from the outside. We are all working together to preserve the natural resources of independent living, that is to say, the support and aid of natural kin; good health; training for remunerative labor; cultivating habits of thrift, and opportunity for self-support.

I think in New Jersey one reason why we enjoy public support of our institutional program, and why there is such wide-spread publicity and public interest in questions of welfare—the big reason is that there have been a few great leaders and prophets, and a Legislature willing to make the right kind of laws. I thank you.

PRESIDENT LOESEL: I know that we have all enjoyed Mrs. Meytrott's address. We are glad that she came over to this State to tell us how they do things over there in New Jersey. We thank you, Mrs. Meytrott.

The next address on the program is to be given by Mr. Charles F. Johnson, Superintendent of the Luzerne County Industrial Home for Boys, at Kis-Lyn.

WORK FOR BOYS

CHARLES F. JOHNSON: I have been very much interested in this address about New Jersey. If I had written the geography, Mrs. Meytrott, before I heard your address, I would have said that New Jersey was the coast line of Pennsylvania over which the bootleggers discharge their cargoes.

If I was writing a history, I would have said that my impression of New Jersey was that it is inhabited with mosquitos that suck your blood, and hotel-keepers who suck your pocketbooks. But my impression of New Jersey has entirely changed. It is worth while and it is good to hear about worth while institutions in a certain State, and I presume that it is interesting to those of other States to hear something of the institutions of our own State.

I want to correct one possible erroneous impression you may have of Pennsylvania when you refer to political gods; we don't have them up here. They all come from the other place.

. For the information of those who are not familiar in the work in which I am interested, I may say I come from a little institution out here in the valley where we endeavor to take the boys who go through our juvenile court of this county and make an effort to build manhood out of boyhood.

Just now we happen to have a population of 235. It is not a large institution at all, and I am rather glad that it isn't, because we are able to do things in small ones that is impossible to do in the large ones. We are just a big family, and when you visit us tomorrow I wish you would bear that in mind. The best thing is the informality of the place, of its home life, because we have the impression that the thing that the boy should have above everything else is the right kind of home life and some corrective training along with that home life.

These increasing social problems that you are dealing with all the time have been intensified, without a doubt, during the last years by the failure of the home. It has probably been complicated by hasty marriages; further involved and tangled by easy divorce.

By making just a hasty glance through the records last week of 222 boys who have come to us, it showed this information:

16 boys have no parents.

82 boys have only one parent (and practically the entire number are below normal.)

124 boys come from not only poor home conditions but from evil home conditions.

Nearly 50 per cent of these boys come from homes where the boy is considered very brilliant if he can pull over the dishonest thing, if you please. A boy who can get away with the thing that is wrong and not be caught is a smart boy in that home.

I think this will be interesting to you: We have at Kis-Lyn, 24 boys coming to us from three families. And at the same time these same families have furnished inmates for girls' institutions, Alms houses and insane asylums.

I know of one particular family from the upper end of this county that has been furnishing inmates for Kis-Lyn ever since its organization, either a cousin or nephew or some one of that brood.

We have, in our occupation, learned of a certain family in this country which, in a very short period of time, has furnished, on the mother's side, more than 1,100 criminals; while on the father's side, in that same period of time, has given this country 476 good citizens.

The same thing has held true with another family that I know of, the Jute family in New York, and also the Golden family in Indiana.

I have thrown out the challenge to friends to study the Price family in Luzerne County, and it has cost this county $25,000 during the last three years, because they are always with us.

At the Reading convention I said to you gentlemen, some of you, (I don't remember the ladies being present at that convention) that I thought we should do certain things. Speaking of the women present at the conventions, I might say that I know of no other scope of work that needs the touch of the feminine hands these days than this particular work. . I think we should welcome women on these Boards. Perhaps it wouldn't be to the liking of all, but I am sure that it is going to be helpful in connection with the problems. I have some radical ideas along those lines.

I was told this afternoon not to call you "Poor Directors," but I think you are all rather poor. It is no disgrace. You have lots of company.

I want to say that if you are a Poor Director in the sense that you don't do your job and do it well, you should get off.

I said at the Reading convention, leaving out every bit of sentiment, and leaving out every bit of slush, economically the thing for this country to do would be to gather up all of the unfit women—and you know the kind of women I am talking about—and segregate and colonize them for the rest of their lives. That would be, economically, the thing to do.

Of course it will cost money. For example, one of the girls from Darlington hadn't been out 60 days until some chap picked her up and married her. What is the result? We are going to have in grand-children what we have had in children.

I repeat that we would be better off economically, leaving out all of the sentiment entirely, if we would segragate and colonize those girls.

I suppose that some of the ladies present might say. "Why not colonize a lot of these men?" There are a lot which ought to be, and a lot worse things should be done to them.

However, it is a fact that the women of your community become the easy prey to the unscrupulous man. That is the reason why I am suggesting this plan.

I want to pass on just a bit to my own particular problem.

I do want to say before I go any farther, I have never gotten over believing, (and I have talked this for 10 years) that all these things all ought to center up in one organization, and under one head in every community. I don't know if it should be the Poor Board—maybe it should—but a dozen different agencies touching the homes is not the thing. There is sure to be a lot of duplication of effort and sentimentality mixed in. Of course we don't want to leave it out, but there is a lot of over-lapping that could be gotten rid of. Don't think that I mean that you fellows ought to run it all. Maybe it should be that some other organization ought to do it, but it ought to be headed up, that is sure.

It doesn't need any elaboration of argument to say this: There are just three or four things which determine what kind of a man the boy will develop into. And these boys do grow so rapidly. You find that true in your own homes. The boys at Kis-Lyn, some of them, have grown up to my shoulders.

To start with, there is his church and all of the other organized activities. But, bless you, do you know that out of 168 hours of a boys life, it is unusual that the church has that boy over 6 hours, and the average church doesn't have him 3 hours. I am a church man and believe thoroughly in it and its activities, but the church activities must get outside of the four walls in order to do her greatest service in regard to her boy life, because the amount of time in the church is so small as compared to the other time he spends outside of the church.

I don't think there is any more conscientious people who are more anxious to solve the problem of the boy and girl than the ministers, the Sunday School teachers and the priests. I don't know of any more honest body of men who are more anxious to be careful to keep their feet solid on the ground than these men.

I may say in passing that I have a lot of faith in our young people. I have a lot of faith in our manhood and womanhood in this country, even at the same time they lose their head and hair. Nevertheless I have a lot of faith in them. I don't know if they are any worse than we were when we were boys. If we had had automobiles and had jazz, we would have been just the way they are today, and not any different. We managed to keep our feet on the ground and our heads out of the clouds, and I am constrained to believe that the young people of today are going to do that thing. Finding fault with them is never going to help the problem. We must have faith in them because they are going to take up these things after we are gone anyway, and we should help them along with the faith we have in them.

The second thing that will mean so much to the boy in later life is his school and its teachers.

Take our public schools today. I think they are better than they ever have been before, and there are better teachers, more educated teachers, better paid, and are competent to cope with the problems of the school today.

They only have a boy 30 hours out of the 168 hours in the week. When I have had the pleasure of talking at teachers' institutes, I always tell them not to be hard and fast with the boys, but to change the boy from one school to another if possible. Sometimes my own managers and matrons feel badly because they are changed, thinking it is a reflection on their ability. A boy may not get along with this school teacher, and he may get along with another one. To the school teachers I say, "Don't wear your feelings on your sleeve. Look ahead a little bit and be willing to try everything to keep the boy in school, and do the best you can for him while he is in school."

I have a lot of faith in our schools.

The third element entering into the matter of the boy's future, is his associates and their amusements.

It would take too long to tell you about some of the boy gangs I have known in Luzerne County. Just today I brought back to Kis-Lyn five boys implicated in robberies that no one would believe if told. They made the robberies at Kingston, and they included the Sinclair Oil Company, the Gem Lunch, private houses, a garage, and other places. I don't know what the amount of the damage was or the amount of goods stolen.

The leader of the gang happened to have been a boy who at one time was with us, and naturally it was not difficult to get the entire story. Implicated all together there were eight boys, and there were their mothers crying and hanging onto their boys. And there were the fathers talking that something was going to be done about it. I felt sure that something would be done because something had to be done.

It was a gang that had been operating for about three months. They had stolen an automobile and had gone off to New York with it. They came back by the way of Scranton, and they acknowledged that they had robbed two places in Scranton.

All of the boys, with the exception of the leader, had homes and parents. The mothers of the boys felt very bad and were there crying. I always feel so sorry for the mothers, and I can't help but pitying the mothers for her boy is just as dear to her as my boy. It makes no difference what kind of a home they have, the kind of language they speak—the conditions don't change that mother love, I can tell you that. She would say, "I didn't know that my boy was going out with these other boys." Of course she didn't!

I am going to tell you something about boys. Every boy belongs to some sort of a gang. It may be the Boy Scouts, a group in a Y.M.C.A., a Sunday School group, or it may be just a little friendly group in the neighborhood. But every boy is going to belong to some kind of a gang, because the gang spirit is something we have to deal with in this country. It is the gang spirit that puts the Rotary Club into action, or the Kiwanis, or the lodge. It is the gang spirit of boys grown into men.

Every gang has a leader, and I am just going to take the time and tell you about two boy gangs. Mr. Bayless is familiar with this I am sure.

Over in Drifton sometime ago there were two rival gangs. I don't know how many boys there were in the two gangs, but the community knew that the gangs were there. They knew all about them.

One day three of them were brought in to us for stealing chickens, and they weren't colored boys either. They would rob the chicken coop and then would go off somewhere and have a feed. Mr. Wilson one night met them coming out with chickens in under their arms. They were going to have a feast somewhere. Three of the boys were brought down to us and they were with us a week. After their hearing it was decided to let them go back home.

I am going to digress just a little bit here, and I am going to state that they were members of the Episcopal church, and their Sunday School teacher was one of the most Godly women on earth.

It seemed as though these gangs had had weekly clashes, and the one gang was told by the leader of the other gang, whose name was Acker, that they should stay out of a certain place, and to stay away from an old buggy. The other gang of course wouldn't do it and would throw sticks and stones at them. Acker went back into the house and got a shotgun. He said, "Now fellows clear out of this place or I will shoot you. This is our fort and if you don't get out I will kill you."

And do you know that when they refused to go, he up and shot the head off of one of the the boys. Of course he skipped. They came to me, and I told them where they might find him. They did and brought him back and put him in jail in Wilkes-Barre. After being in jail some unscrupulous attorney tried to make out that the boy didn't know the gun was loaded.

I was asked by the court to get the truth and I spent some time trying to get the correct information. I learned that the boy actually loaded the gun and killed the boy. The boy was sent to Huntingdon and so far as I know he is doing well, although he is not there now.

Now the thought is this: Everybody up in Drifton knew of those gangs, and nobody took any interest in trying to direct those boys aright, with the result of that terrible thing. However it was a thing that might be expected, for this gang of boys one time robbed a place of 48 revolvers. Now wouldn't you expect, under the leadership of Acker, that this gang would start something where some one would get hurt. Of course those things must be expected.

The last in the list of elements that enter into what is going to make a boy into a man, is the home, his parents, his family.

You know, a lot of homes are not much more than "places." They are merely places where they eat and sleep, where there is no regularity of any kind of home life. The boys come and go more or less at will, with the result that there is not that influence there that should be in the home, the right influence of the mother and father. And in cases where the boy doesn't have a mother or father, and perhaps has a step-mother or step-father of the wrong kind, it is exceedingly difficult for the boy to get the right training in that home.

I don't know how much we may depend upon heredity.

There is a little story about a little girl who had come home from school, and it so happened that her mother and father had had a spat, as sometimes fathers and mothers do. They had had a little bit of a quarrel, and the father was sitting back behind a newspaper, and the mother sat over her sewing. The child said to her mother, "Mother, we are studying whether or not people descended from monkeys. Did we come from monkeys?"

The mother said, "Mary I don't know. I never knew your father's people."

Every boy, who has gone through what I have been talking to you about, has in addition to the complications of our present day home life certain kinds of amusements as he goes about in his community.

We are living in a new age and in these communities the people haven't been able to keep pace with their children. I want to tell you that the average foreign family doesn't know the present day life as their children know it. They don't know anything about the temptations which their children are subjected to, and I have a lot of sympathy for those parents who don't understand and who have been unable to keep pace with the times.

And then there is the increase of crime in this country. During the last 18 years crime has increased 12 times over. I am not an alarmist about those things, because it seems that we have so much money for the people to steal, that we have a lot left.

Seven per cent of the population of this country is composed of boys between 12 and 18 years of age. This seven per cent of our population furnishes now 60 per cent of our criminals. In fifteen years the average of the criminals of this country has decreased ten years, until the average age of men in our penitentiaries is now under 25 years of age; whereas fifteen years ago it was slightly under 35 years of age.

I might go farther and tell you that tonight, down there what we call Cherry Hill, there are 421 boys in the penitentiary under 21 years of age—mere boys. I might go farther and tell you that the cost to the State of Pennsylvania annually is $10,000,000, and this does not include the salaries of officers, judges and court expenses. The annual cost of crime in the United States exceeds the income of the National Government in any single year.

I am telling you these things because I think the battle line of this thing is back there in the teens when we have those boys and girls in the home.

I wonder if we will ever get back to the time when we will be able to occupy the time of our children. I think the water spigot is a curse to us, because when I was a boy I had to carry water. I think the electric light is a curse to us, for when I was a boy I had to clean lamps. I think the gas stove is a curse to us, for when I was a boy I had to chop and carry in the wood.

Tell me tonight what the boy of today does? He doesn't do anything! Why? Because there isn't anything for him to do. Tell me what you have your boy at home do. I think he ought to be occupied.

I am a father of two boys and I have had a chance to make a study of this question. About all the boys of today do is study their lessons, shine their shoes, perhaps, and pick up their clothes, and learn to wash back of their ears.

Today all that you have to do is to turn a spigot; press a button. Tell me what there is for the boys to do?

I am not critical of the things on the part of the parents, for I don't know what to do to keep the boy occupied. I do think we are doing a lot better in some directions than we used to.

One day there was a little girl and her mother riding on the train, and sitting directly in front of them was one of these fellows who carries a cane, and sometimes sucks it without any sugar on the end of it. And the little girl said to her mother, "Mother, did you tell me that God made everybody?"

The mother said, "Yes dear, I did."

"Well, mother, did God make that?"

"Yes, dear, God made that."

"Did God make me?"

"Yes, yes."

And then the little girl said, "Mother, I believe God is doing better work than he used to."

I am inclined to think, with all of the efforts we put forth, the fact that we know about these things is a good indication that we are doing better work. Some people think that it is foolish and that the boy should be thrashed and sent to bed without his supper. Some people don't believe as you do at all.

It is like the man who was riding on the street car and he sat next to a preacher. The preacher was sitting there reading the newspaper. This man who sat next to him was a sort of soap-box orator, and he turned to the preacher and said to him, "I don't believe in the church."

The preacher merely said "Very well", and kept on reading his paper.

Pretty soon the man said again to the preacher, "I don't believe in the church."

The preacher said, "Very well."

And then a little later the fellow again said to the preacher, "I don't believe in the church."

The preacher replied, "Go to hell then."

As I say, there are a lot of people who don't believe in the things that you do. I just want to say to you to go ahead and do the things anyhow because you are trying to do the things that are worth while.

. I don't know if you have ever heard the story about the fellow who had had a little too much drink, and he came home and tried to find the keyhole. Finally he did, and he entered the hall. He tried to get up the stairs and as he neared the top he saw something all dressed in white. His wife had dressed up like a ghost thinking she could scare him so that he would not drink any more.

He said, "Who are you?"

The answer came back, "I am the devil."

A chill came over him at first and then he stuck out his hand and said, "I am so glad to see you. I married your sister."

But the next morning she got even with him. She said at the breakfast table, "Say John, I had a funny dream last night. I dreamed of a ladder which reached up to heaven, and every one who was to ascend that ladder was given a piece of chalk. They were to mark on each rung of the ladder as they went up every mean thing they had done during their life. I dreamed that I started to go up and had only gotten up six or seven rungs when down came some one as fast as they could, and would you believe it, it was you. I said to you, 'What are you coming down for?' You replied,

'I am coming down for more chalk."

I just want to say this in closing: It is worth while to do anything we can today to help youth keep its feet on the ground.

I remember when I lived out West there was quite a sensation, one which would not be so great today, but it was at that time. One night one of the wealthiest men of Omaha got into a buggy and drove to a place on the outskirts of the city. He drove an old gray horse, and he took with him $20,000 in gold coins. He drove out over Douglas Street, and you know how beautiful that street is, those of you who are acquainted in Omaha. He drove back over there to a cottonwood tree, two miles out, and placed the bag of gold down into the tree and drove back. He had been told by the Pinkerton detectives not to do it, for Mr. Cudahy, the big meat packer, had received a note stating, "If you leave $20,000 in gold at Baker's Corners your boy will be returned to you safely before daylight."

He did it, and he would have done it had it been for $200,000. Pat Crowe and his accomplices had kidnapped his 17-year old boy and threatened to kill him unless the money was forthcoming. Of course they were apprehended later, but I want to bring out this fact: The reason that Mr. Cudahy was willing to put that money there was because it was his boy.

I want you to remember that every boy is some father's and some mother's boy, and remember that we haven't done our full duty until we have thrown around every boy and every girl all of the safeguards at our command. I thank you.

PRESIDENT LOESEL: I am sure that we are all glad that we were present tonight, and I am sorry that the others could not have been present and heard these two very fine addresses.

ADJOURNMENT

WEDNESDAY MORNING SESSION
October 5, 1927

The meeting convened at 8:45 o'clock, President Charles F. Loesel presiding.

PRESIDENT LOESEL: We will now come to order please.

The invocation will be made by Rabbi A. S. Anspacher, of Beth Israel Temple, Hazleton, Pa.

... The invocation was made by Rabbi Anspacher at this time ...

PRESIDENT LOESEL: We will now have any reports which are to be presented.

MR. A. G. GRAHAM: Mr. Chairman, I would like to make a report of the Auditing Committee at this time.

... Mr. Graham made a brief report at this time ...

... Upon motion duly made and seconded the report of the Auditing Committee was received. Motion carried ...

PRESIDENT LOESEL: Mr. Mackin, have you a report to present at this time?

MR. D. A. MACKIN: Mr. President, the report is not ready to present at this time, but if you have a few minutes to spare we have an old question which should be revived.

You will recall during the last two sessions of the Legislature a bill was passed, with the approval of this Association, with the unanimous backing of this Association, creating a retirement pension fund for employees at district institutions. This bill covered already what is and has been in force in regard to similar work. The original bill was sponsored by Senator Joyce, of Luzerne County and passed the Senate and House, and was vetoed by Governor Pinchot, the reason given being that it was unsound in construction.

The point made was that there was an arbitrary figure fixed of 2 per cent of the employees earnings, or monthly wage, not to exceed $4, and it permitted no leeway in the way of increase, if that shouldn't be sufficient.

They evidently lost sight of this fact, that the 2 per cent was only part of the fund, and that the law further permitted and authorized Directors of the Poor, and others, as heads and trustees of mental hospitals, and other institutions, to appropriate from their funds sufficient to cover any amount necessary, so that the argument that it is functionally unsound won't stand.

After the veto of the first bill, the convention again formally approved unanimously this bill, and it was presented before the Legislature. The bill was submitted to a number of attorneys and authorities on constitutional law and those familiar with insurance, with the idea that any change might be made so as to cover the objections. Our own Legislative Committee, together with the others to whom it was submitted, said, "No change is necessary. It is all right."

The bill was again submitted and it passed the House and Senate, and together with other bills went into the hands of the Governor. It was one of the 800 bills in his hands at the end of the last session, and of course Governor Fisher announced that he would be unable to give hearings on all of these bills, and suggested that a brief be filed.

At a meeting of the Executive Committee, held in Hazleton in April, the matter was brought to the attention of the members of the Executive Committee. The bill was then before Governor Fisher. I suggested that a brief be filed. We called in a stenographer and dictated the matter and filed the brief which contained what we thought was an unanswerable argument in favor of the bill.

However, the bill was vetoed again on the same ground.

What I want to bring to your attention is the fact that during the last session, bill No. 157, was passed, which is a bill creating a pension of employees of Third Class Cities.

This bill is an absolute copy in every particular of the bill that was vetoed, with the exception that it was a little different in the formation of the trustee organization, in that the mayor and two members of the commissioners are part of the Board. Our Board is formed by appointment of the court.

I wanted to suggest that the Resolutions Committee make a note of this again and that it again be formally approved. And I would also suggest that in the printed proceedings of this convention that the two bills be printed in parallel columns, to show the likeness of this bill that we are endeavoring to put through. A very great number of people have spoken to me about the bill since our last convention, and I would urge that we again get behind this bill. I thank you.

PRESIDENT LOESEL: Are there any other remarks on this subject? If not, we will have the report of the Committee on Officers.

... The report was presented and the follow ing Officers were duly elected:

President:

    Charles L. Huston, Chester County.

Vice Presidents:

    T. C. White, Mercer County.

    Mrs. Sue Willard, Indiana County.

    Dr. J. E. Waaser, Carbon County.

    Caspar M. Titus, Philadelphia County.

    Mrs. E. C. Dunn, Montgomery County.

    John S. Hamberg, Westmoreland County.

    S. H. Boyd, Lancaster County.

Secretary:

> Harry A. Jones, Esq., Washington County.

Assistant Secretaries:

> Mrs. Jackson S. Schultz, Elk County.
>
> W. W. Dight, Mercer County.

Treasurer:

> D. A. Mackin, Luzerne County.

Honorary Secretaries:

> E. D. Solenberger, Philadelphia County.
>
> T. Springer Todd, Fayette County.

**

PRESIDENT LOESEL: The next will be the report of the Committee on Place.

... The report of the Committee on Place was presented, Philadelphia having been chosen as the next convention city ...

MR. R. C. BUCHANAN: Mr. President, I move that the report of the Committee on Place be accepted and referred to the Executive Committee with power to act.

... The motion was seconded and carried ...

MR. T. C. WHITE: Mr. President, Ladies and Gentlemen: We are all aware that our Secretary, who has served us these many years faithfully and economically, has resigned, and while he is not severing his connections entirely, yet through the pressure of work in other fields he feels that he cannot continue as Secretary of this Association.   .

There has been a committee of Mr. Graham, Mr. Plankington, Mr. McLaughlin, and myself, who have put it upon our shoulders to act in the capacity of a committee to gather together funds for a little remembrance to this gentlemen who has served us so faithfully. We wish to present him with a little token of respect, so that in after years when his hair begins to turn gray, he will look upon this token as having been presented to him from the members of this Association out of respect for his untiring efforts. If any of the members wish to contribute to this fund, kindly see any member of this committee.

MR. W. J. TREMBATH: I have been reminded that the Committee on Officers failed to assign the salaries of the Secretary and Treasurer, and I move that the salaries of these officers be the same as last year.

... The motion was seconded and carried ...

... Upon motion duly made and seconded, Mr. Solenberger was given a rising vote of thanks for his long service to the Association ...

SECRETARY SOLENBERGER: I wish to say to you that I treasure most of all the thought that is back of each one of the suggestions and resolutions that have been made touching myself. To every man and to every woman who is here in this Association, I want to express my appreciation.

It means much to me for what little I have done to see the increasing interest manifested here on the part of the representatives of the sixty-seven counties of Pennsylvania, who are trying to solve the problems for which this organization came into existence.

I want to say that the greatest satisfaction in connection with the matter is the growth in numbers. I can well remember when Mr. Mackin was President during the Reading Convention in 1915, at which time they honored me with the office of Secretary. At that time there were only a few present. The growth in attendance, and the increasing interest in the work, is to me, Mr. Chairman, the greatest satisfaction.

I don't feel that I am leaving. I expect to continue to attend, for you have honored me with the position of Honorary Secretary, and it will be my greatest pleasure to work with your new officers in future years.

I believe I told you that since 1907 I have missed only one session, in 1922, at which time Mr. Trembath was President, and the doctor wouldn't let me go away from home on account of the flu.

I want to say again that I do treasure the thought you have expressed and I do want to thank you for it. I can't say anything about Mr. White's suggestion. It is a bit embarrassing. But I do appreciate the thought that has prompted it.

Just one more word with regard to the new officers. I sincerely hope that you will give them the same cooperation that you have given me. Mr. Huston, who has been a Director in Chester County for 20 years, is going to make a fine President. I want to express my personal congratulations to him, and also congratulate the Association that we are to have his services as President.

I trust that Mr. Huston will pardon me if I refer to the fact that he has been active in many good works. In the church he has been a distinguished layman and an active force. He has been a free giver from his own purse to many different kinds of private charities, and I believe that the Association is most fortunate that we have for the coming year Mr. Huston as our President.

It seems to me that we are entering a new era in Pennsylvania, and that we have great things in store for us. Let us work together unitedly for the further success of our work in every department represented in the convention. I thank you.

PRESIDENT LOESEL: I know that we are all sorry to lose Mr. Solenberger as our Secretary. I am sure that Mr. Jones will make a good Secretary.

The next on the program will be an address by Dr. C. C. Carstens, Director, Child Welfare League of America. His subject is "Community Program for Child Care."

COMMUNITY PROGRAM FOR CHILD CARE
Dr. C. C. Carstens, New York

I have an unusual pleasure in coming back to Pennsylvania where I undertook my first social work, not to begin with in child care, but certainly not very far away from it. The lessons I have learned since leaving the social work of Pennsylvania, are practically those which could be built, and were built, on the experience which I obtained here in this State about 25 years ago.

I have been in the field of Child Welfare now for about 20 years, and in the work now placed in my hands I come in contact with the Child Welfare work in a good many States.

I would indeed be foolish if I thought that what could be done in North Carolina, New York, or Massachusetts could immediately be clapped onto another State, whether it be Pennsylvania, Louisiana, or California. I think there are certain lessons and certain trends in the development of child care that are part of the thinking, part of the experiences of the nation, and of the various States. It is true that what would particularly fit Montgomery County today, might perhaps not fit Allegheny or Beaver Counties.

It is none the less true that there is a general scheme of Child Welfare work that is worth while to think about, and on the basis of that experience in other counties, and in other States, we can perhaps learn some lesson. It is from that standpoint that I accepted the invitation that Mr. Solenberger sent to me some months ago to be with you today.

Whether or not I have anything to give you, it remains with you rather than with me. I hope you will attempt to apply the few things that I · may be able to say to you to your own tasks. However they will not fit in every case.

It reminds me of Mary, who was asked, "Mary, did you entertain a man in the kitchen last night?"

Mary replied, "Well that is for him to say."

When we come to study the whole field of Child Welfare, there are certain things that stand out pretty positively, not only in Pennsylvania, but in a great many other States.

Sometimes, shooting as fast as I have to from one State to another, it is a little embarrassing to keep up with developments. I think during the last three years I have done work in all of the States in the Unite States, with the exception of Nevada. That, I think, is rather a splendi record, for I have had to be in my office in New York part of the tim Not a great deal.

One of the things that stands out more positively than any other single fact is that we believe now more in the family than we used to, in its various applications. One of those applications is the question of how we can help to maintain the right kind of family home, because if there is any single fact in the lives of us, it is that we belong to some family, and we treasure it with mighty few exceptions.

It is the sense of belonging to the family, even though sometimes it wasn't quite up to the highest grade. You know, and I know, that in spite of weaknesses we see fine men and women come out of those families, and they prize them just the same.

That is a fundamental fact in child care, that nothing can take the place after all of the child's own family, if there is something left to be built upon. There are some cases where there is nothing left, just a shell. But let us not be too sure about that.

I presume that I have taken as large a part in the breaking up of family life as any single person here, in spite of what I say. I was for 14 years in charge of the Massachusetts Society for the Prevention of Cruelty to Children, and we had from 1,200 to 1,500 cases in court every year. I know what I speak of, when I say I have taken part in breaking up family life. But I have become increasingly cautious about it, because the better I knew the family the more things I found that were worth something, rather than the fewer things I found that were not. Always, of course, there were exceptions.

I assure you there are certain conditions that cannot be remedied except by the most drastic means, but it is the person who makes the slight contact that sees only the weaknesses. It is those who study carefully what the main-springs of action in the lives of families are after all who see the strength.

That is the foundation upon which Mother's Assistance Funds are built. Family life is the most precious thing, and you men and women are the ones who are assisting families over the hard spots so that they may be kept as families, rather than to be scattered here and there.

I have said that it is the most outstanding thing in my experience, and it is for that reason, friends, when we come to study the problems of child placing work, the same facts underlie the development that is going on at the present time.

I have no objection to good institutional work for children, but on the whole certainly the tendency is in the other direction, because of the fact, as I have mentioned, we are coming to prize the values of the family itself.

During the time I was in Massachusetts, where family placement is a common and almost the universal thing, I saw fewer of the values of institutional life. But I have since that time seen some splendid institutional work, and have seen some very shoddy home placement work. I am not talking about Pennsylvania, but if the shoe fits, put it on.

However, the underlying thought is the value of the family. That brings me to some important limitations, it seems to me, in connection with the care of children outside of their own homes.

We used to place children on suspicion, and the thing would work all right. Perhaps we didn't think it was suspicion, but as we look back upon it, it couldn't be very much else. We depended upon human nature, that human nature and kindness in everybody, in greater or lesser degree, after all, give the child a chance.

We didn't pay very much attention to the fact that we ought to know more about the family in which this child was placed. We didn't pay a great deal of attention to the question whether the family in which it was placed was just the right kind of a family into which this particular child would fit. We did say that this family had a nice home, and everything looked all right. Perhaps they had a piano, and a nice rug, nice furniture, etc., and we understood that the family had a good reputation in the community. It seemed that that was all that was necessary.

And then comes the next point I want to bring out in the scheme of child care. We must know our children! Otherwise we cannot provide well for them when it is necessary for them to slip out of their own homes and possibly have to be placed in an entirely different home and different environment.

That is the next most fundamental thing in the scheme of child care—that we may know our children better.

I think I ought to repeat a story which I have told previously in Pennsylvania. Perhaps several times I have told this story, but I think not many in this audience have heard it.

One day there came a telephone message to the office, asking if we were willing to receive into the Shelter Home, of which I had charge, a small boy. He was then about seven years old. I will call him Henry, and that was his real name. These were the facts as they were brought out:

Henry lived in a community of about 100,000 people, some fifty odd miles away from our Central Office, and at the age of five he had already become rather a spry lad. He climbed into an open window of a nice residence at the age of six, and without the family knowing it, slipped into the upstairs guest chamber and fixed himself up all cozy and nice and slept until morning without the family knowing that he had been in the house. Of course he wanted to get away, and he also wanted them to understand that he had been there. As he went across the hall and out the front door he gave an unearthly yell so as to let them know that something had happened.

It was early in the morning and the folks were just getting up. They heard the yell and when they went to the door they saw a kid running off down the street. They discovered that he had been in the house but did not see that he had destroyed anything, only had slept in the best room in one of the finest homes in the city.

These people called up the police and told them of the incident. They said, "It sounds as though that might have been Henry." In other words, Henry had a reputation.

It wasn't long until the police concluded that he was not likely to be a very useful citizen and that they had better get their hands on him as quickly as possible. He had helped himself to fruit, and also had drunk the milk from bottles standing on porches, and a great many other things, and at the age of seven he was in court most of the time. Before that it was impossible to bring him into court, he being only six years of age.

At the age of five his mother had taken him to school, and wanted to share him with the teachers, but in some way it didn't please the teacher, and it was decided that Henry was just as well off out of school until he was six years old.

I presume that you know of a lad similar to Henry. I have had a great many people come up to me and tell me, "I have a Henry in my own family."

Well, Henry was before the courts at the age of seven. The police had all the evidence needed to send him to your Glen Mills, or to some other institution as a delinquent. He had committed plenty of depredations and the judge was about to send him away because it seemed the only thing to do. The mother and father were there. They had thrown up their hands, not knowing what to do with him.

As the judge was about to send him away to some school, my agent stepped forward and out of kindness of heart, she said, "Don't you want me to have Henry for a little while?"

The judge didn't want to send him away, but it seems that it was the last resort. He said, "Yes, we will continue the case for two weeks, but you had better take him to Dr. Wallace."

Dr. Wallace is in charge of an institution for feeble-minded, not far away, I think 12 miles away from the place, where she might go on the way up to the Shelter Home where the boy was to be taken care of temporarily. It was the suggestion of the judge that Henry might be feeble-minded.

Of course they fell in with the plan, and Dr. Wallace heard part of what I have told you. He said, "There is evidently something the matter with Henry but it is not feeble-mindedness. You had better take him to Dr. so and so, (suggesting the name of an eminent psychiatrist in the city of Boston.")

We took him to this doctor and asked him if he would see what he could find. He was very glad to make a careful analysis, which was based on a good many scientific discoveries and understandings of child nature, together with a very wide experience.

After he had talked a few minutes with Henry, Henry decided that he wouldn't answer any other questions. Henry understood court and the police, and all of those things, and he understood school. Those were part of his experience, but this was a new thing and he decided that he wouldn't play. When the doctor asked him a certain question, Henry would merely grunt. The doctor decided to go no further.

On the way out Henry had helped himself to the doctor's stop-watch which had been lying on the table, and carried it off to the Shelter Home where he was to stay for a few days. He had it pretty well under way as to getting it apart before it was discovered that the watch had been taken.

I am giving you these details to show you the kind of lad we were dealing with.

Two days later Henry once more went to the doctor, taking with him the remains of this fine stop-watch. Previous to our going, I did what you or anybody else would do, and that was to rake Henry over the coals and tell him what sort of a useless youngster he was, and that he ought to reform—and all sorts of useless advice.

That isn't the way the doctor dealt with him at all. He was intent upon finding out what was in this boy's head, rather than giving him bits of useless advice.

The boy had returned the stop-watch in a somewhat dilapidated condition, and the doctor made this episode the avenue, the open door by which he got into the boy's makeup, the way the boy was thinking and acting, and he was taken off his guard.

Henry expected heaven to fall upon him, but instead of that he was being studied in a perfectly natural way. He was not being studied by feeling his bumps, but the doctor was finding out what he was thinking about and what he was doing and likely to do in other situations. The outcome was they got on splendid terms, without Henry noticing anything unusual.

The doctor said to Henry, "Maybe you would like a few of my puzzles too," and he brought out his form board, etc. He knew the lad by this time, within a space of three or four hours. He gave him a few tests just to confirm it. Henry was then turning seven and the doctor gave him five tests that would apply to a six-year old child, and Henry did them right off the bat. And then he was given some tests for a seven-year old child, and Henry did those just the same as the others. And then he was given tests for an eight-year old child, and Henry did those equally as easy as he had done the others.

The doctor now gave Henry five tests for a nine-year old child and Henry did those. And then Henry did four of the five tests that applied to the ten-year old child. But Henry couldn't do the tests for the eleven-year old child.

In other words, Henry had an intelligence quotient of 147. It was quite aside from the fact that the judge was of the opinion that Henry was to make his own life, to live his own life and develop his own activities.

Now the family from which Henry came was a decent one, and they were not dependent upon the Directors of the Poor or any organization in the community. They had lived a decent life, but the Lord had given them (I don't know how and you don't either) one of the four children who was a super-normal child. The school had been closed to him, and the police said, "We will get that little devil yet," and the mother had thrown up her hands. The mother had enough to do taking care of the other children and Henry just managed himself and his own affairs. · She did the best she could under the circumstances. Henry managed· his own affairs, and did it pretty poorly.

It is comparatively easy to find out what the situation is when you have a man or woman carefully trained for the purpose of understanding child life and child nature. Then comes the question, "What shall we do about it?" That is another story, isn't it?

The doctor called me over to his office and told me the whole story after he had made his analysis, and I, of course, was very much interested: I asked him the question that I just mentioned, "What are we going to do about it?" After all, that is what social work means. Psychology may stop with an analysis, but social work must go on and we must work out a method. Otherwise it isn't going to be worth very much to the community.

This doctor is just as much of a social worker as he is a psychiatrist, because he goes further than that. That is where he has obtained very valuable information and has gained vast experience.

The upshot of the matter was, finally he said, "It is practically up to us to determine whether Henry is going to be one of the most clever criminals Massachusetts has ever had, or one of the brightest citizens that the State may enjoy." ·

And then he went on, "If we are wise enough to work the problem out we can make Henry into a good citizen." ·

I said, "Well, he has to live somewhere. Can't he go back to his own family? They are good people."

He said, "I don't know, but I will send for the boy's parents." ·

The father and mother came. They were not particularly endowed with riches, but they had decent conveniences of life, and besides that they had decent ideas and wanted to do what they could with the lad. They were not very intelligent, but none the less they were pleased that something was going to be done with the boy, and they appreciated that something had to be done. Of course they wanted him at home if at all possible, but they were willing to do what was right.

After carefully considering the matter, and getting their full cooperation, it was decided that Henry would not prosper just at the present time at home. It was learned that it would be impossible to change their whole attitude at home right off the bat, where Henry had been told all of the time not to do this, not to do that, and the mother was not satisfied until Henry was safely tucked into bed and asleep.

It was decided that if Henry was to be really developed into the kind of lad you and I would want to see him develop into, he must, for a time at least, have that kind of training that would perhaps fit him so that he could once again return to his home and his community. :

I said, "Well, if he can't return home, why can't he go to the institution into which he was about to go?"

The doctor said, "No, no, that won't do! That won't do at all. That may fit other boys, but it will not fit this boy."

Here was this boy just turning seven years old, and he had a quotient of 147. The doctor said that he would absorb the things he would learn from the older boys and get into bad habits. The doctor said, "Henry needs to be insulated."

I said, "Insulated?"

He said, "Yes, he needs that current activity guiding him so that he can't shoot off in all directions. He must run into a path that will gradually get under control."

I said, "Well, how are you going to insulate him? He can't go to the family or institution, you say?"

We came to the decision that he must be placed into another family, a family intelligent enough and experienced enough and patient enough to take care of Henry.

It is a long story, but may I just tell you, after 16 families had been visited to find the right one, the right one was finally found. These families were not merely visited, but they were studied to determine whether they had all of those qualities I mentioned. That is where Henry could be insulated, in family life.

I just want to call your attention to the fact that you and I, as we are getting this experience in our respective communities, will find resources that we never dreamed of in families where we thought those things never existed.

After all the biggest problem of child care is solved in families and not in institutions. The institutions supplement, and they supplement well, but they are not to supplant our individual families. If we will assist in finding the right family, then we will have solved the problem.

It is in the insulation, and that is made possible only in family life. That is the third most important point that I would like to leave with you this morning—the family life is the way of solving a great many problems that formerly we didn't think could be solved in that way.

It doesn't do any good to look at my watch, for it stopped as soon as I got to Hazleton. I don't know whether to quit now or not, but will you pardon me if I go on just a few minutes more?

There is a fourth factor that I would like to speak of; yes, there are two more.

Institutional care in children, as I said a few moments ago, is a fine supplement for family home care. And I have already told you that I don't believe in family home care that isn't the right kind of family home care. It has to be of a pretty good grade for me to have anything to do with it.

But institutional care is changing, and that is also a factor of great importance. I can name you an institution in the United States (and this one doesn't happen to be in Pennsylvania) where the superintendent of the institution said, "I will not take any child into my institution for care that doesn't belong there." ·

Think of the heresy connected with a statement like that! Usually we take them in on suspicion, and we have a bed that we would like to fit them into. But here is a man who first wants to make a careful analysis of the situation and see whether or not that child really is going to be benefitted by being placed in this institution. And if not in that one, perhaps some other one. I wonder if he is right in this respect?

In other words we are getting down to the fundamentals, and we are finding out what our institutions can do for this child, and not merely look upon it with the thought, "There is another bed vacant into which this child can be slipped." In other words the institutional care is becoming a part of the scheme in child care, in that they are asking themselves, "Does Mary fit in here?" or "Does John belong here?" And they may come to the conclusion that they do not fit in that particular institution, and are placed somewhere else.

In other words, the foster home is the alternative of the institution, and the institution is the alternative of the foster home. However, a complete analysis of the case on either side is the watch-word now-a-days. We make a social inquiry, a medical inquiry and a psychological inquiry as we think it is necessary, and the basis of this analysis decides whether it is better for the child to be placed in an institution or a family.

It should not be determined on the thought, "Here is a nice institution," because the benefit we are after is the direct benefit to the child nature with whom you are dealing. In other words it is a scientific basis, rather than a merely sentimental basis.

And for that reason institutional care is changing. It is getting married to "child placement." They are marching along together, instead of pulling each other's hair. That is going on increasingly in this State and in others.

Not more than a year ago we had an opportunity from my office to make a study of the population of a rather small church institution in Pennsylvania. The study of that population indicated that there were children there in that church institution from five different states, and of the 33 children that were there, after we had presented the facts to that Board of Trustees—all intelligent men and women—seven of those children needed that institutional care. The other 26 children it was determined should not be there.

Now that didn't mean that the institution wasn't giving the proper care to those children, but it meant that those children needed a complete change.

Have I given you number four? If I haven't, I will sum it up in this way: Child Welfare and Institutional work are both finding their spheres. One other point and then I am through.

Formerly Social Agencies just grew up like Topsy. Somebody had a few ideas and wanted to do something for the community in which he lived. He perhaps left something in the way of worldly gifts because he wanted to contribute something to the life of the community. He had an idea. What did he do? He built an Old Ladies Home, or usually a Children's Home.

That was a nice thing to do, but did he inquire whether it was needed or not? No, that would be heresy!

Let me tell you a true story:

About 20 years ago a gentlemen in the Middle West decided that he wanted to do something for his community. About 20 years ago he made a will stating that the rest of his estate should go for the care of children, to be cared for up to the age of self-supporting. I will name the city. It was the city of Flint, Michigan.

Flint, in the census of 1920 had the largest growth of any city in the United States, with the exception of Akron, Ohio. It being a large automobile center, Flint had the largest growth, with the exception of Akron.

When his will was probated, there were some complications. This was no reflection upon him, or anybody else, but when the will was probated five years ago it was found that he had left the nice little sum of $800,000 for this Children's Home, where the children were to be kept until they were self-supporting. This was left to St. Paul's Episcopal Church in the city of Flint, Michigan.

The vestry of that church was asked, according to the will, to organize itself into a Board of Trustees and build the home.

It chanced in the organization of that Board of Trustees, they chose for the president of that Board a man of very large affairs, and in my judgment, and I believe in your judgment, a very wise man.

In a roundabout way he came to our office and said, "We have $800,000 with which to build a home. I don't want to build this home unless the city of Flint needs it."

I once more say to you that is the so-called present day social heresy to say a thing like that. Think of a church receiving $800,000 to build a home with and then not go to work and build it, whether the community needed it or not. That would be called heresy.

I will say that it was very unusal, but it happened this way: To this man himself, $800,000 meant little, for he was a multi-millionaire. He wasn't impressed with the amount in the least. You and I would be. I am sure I would be.

He asked us to make a study of the needs of the city of Flint. He said this: "If we don't need this Children's Home, I wouldn't load upon a community a thing that later on will be pointed to with discredit, and will not be a credit to Mr. Whaley."

We came to the conclusion, after a careful study, having sent one of my assistances down there at their expense, that it was not needed. It developed that there were two Children's Homes there and neither one of them ever filled.   And also there was a Child Placing Agency, and·the Children's Aid Society has a county branch there.

We recommended that they didn't need it, and they certainly didn't need it.   But we said, "You need something else in child care, and we hope that you can do that."

What did they need?   They needed what I will call a Diagnostic Receiving Home for the children of that county, Flint being the county seat, so that it might become the center of things and might enrich the life and activity of all of the different Children's Agencies of that County.

Mr. Mark, the chairman who was pleased with our recommendation, said, "That is what we want."

Ladies and gentlemen, we want to be able to be of service to the schools, to the courts, to the Children's Agencies, and to the citizens.   We want to be of assistance to those people who have Henrys, I will say.   We want to be of assistance to those families who have social problems within the family which will quickly become community problems if not solved, although they may be highly respected people and people of intelligence.

I said to this man, "I am very glad that you feel that way, but this is a will and you can't change that."

He said, "No, that is true, but I will put my lawyer to work on it, on the basis of your brief and we will go to the courts and have that will re-interpreted."

This man, who is next to the President of the General Motors Company of America, was in a position to do things, and generally when they want to do a thing they get it done.   I don't mean in any improper way, but I mean they know how to go about it in order to get things done.   In social work we haven't as yet learned that trick.

His lawyer wrote a brief and this was the analysis of it, and I will give it to you for what it is worth.   Of course I can't repeat it verbatim, but this is about what it covered:

"Mr. Whaley, twenty years ago, wanted to make a will which would benefit his community.   Possibly the things he wanted to do were needed twenty years ago, but we have learned this, and this, and this, and we believe it is not needed now.   After receiving expert advice, it has been proven that it is not needed, and if Mr. Whaley were here we feel sure that he wouldn't want to do this.   He isn't here and in plain words we want to change this will to read in such a manner that it will be possible to do the thing that Flint needs now."

The court was willing to insert a little phrase that made it possible to do the thing that was needed in 1927, for that building was completed in July of this year, and is now in use as the center of service to all of the people of that whole county and of that community.

Public service is not different from private service in· its essentials. Yes, it is different!   I have never been in public service, but at this minute.

I have 700 public wards under my care in the city of Rochester, N. Y., where a Children's Aid Society was severely criticised. I have some of the best people at work up there now, and some of them received their experience in Philadelphia. They are working that problem out.

In its foundation there is no difference. Yes, there are essential differences in the way you can do the thing, but on the whole, friends, whether it is a public unit or private, these various services I refer to do not figure quite as important, but yet they must be done in every community.

In certain parts of the United States they are being done privately, and in some other parts they are being done publicly.

My feeling is that there is such an interlinking of public and private service necessary now-a-days, and that it is linked together advantageously in every community when we analyze the situation. It is not so much what the jobs are, but rather what we should do. The thought is, "What can I do?" And also, "What can the other fellow do?"

As I said before, formerly they all grew up on sentimental bases, but now we have come to acknowledge the fact that we have a workable plan, and that public and private have parts to play, working side by side, working out these questions together.

I believe that the county is the most important unit in the development of the child care program in the United States.

I didn't grow up in Massachusetts; I was an imported product. I came from the Middle West, and stopped for a while in Philadelphia, and marched further on. In Massachusetts they don't know what a county is. In almost all parts of the United States the county is the unit of service that really has to be depended upon to do the work.

Public service is the foundation finally, and that will be different in Massachusetts, Pennsylvania, or California, because there is a different method used and people think differently along those lines. We have 48 different representatives working this experiment out, and some have gotten along fine, but finally the unit of service in my judgment, as I have previously said, is the county.

Therefore, the problem of child care is finally largely in your hands, because the program must rest upon the shoulders of the Directors of the Poor and other public agencies. Yes, and also the private agencies, for they sometimes do a great deal, and many times better, for they have fewer limitations. However, finally the job rests with you.

I was interested very much two years ago, having been chosen as one of the judges to decide which city in the State of Wisconsin was the best city in which to bring up children. I was chairman of the Board of Judges. There were 10 of us brought in for that purpose. I represented the Social Welfare, and there were other activities represented. There was a judge on Industry, a judge on Health, a judge on City Planning, a judge on Education, etc. There were 10 different phases, all having their part to play in the scheme of child care.

What part does industry have to play? It has a very important part to play. The city of Kenosha was the city finally decided upon. And why particularly was Kenosha picked out as being the best city in which to raise children?

There was a fine industry there, and some of you know what it is. I am not an advertiser of the Nash car, but I speak of the plant where the Nash cars are manufactured.

This company had built splendid homes for their men who were working in their plant, homes that were not merely comfortable, but were artistic. They made it possible that these homes could be purchased, which gave an impetus to the social work.

There is another fine works there, that of the Simmons Bed Company. They also have taken an interest in their people, and these industries were back of that whole child-care program. Instead of building a Children's Home, as fine as that is, they said, "Let us see what we can do." They did it!

In other words, the program of child care is the whole program of the community, and that is the contribution that must be made, public and private, in the work that we finally have to do. We must see that the youngster gets his chance, the youngster that you are taking care of in your own homes, but if he gets beyond you, then the community will step in and do its part. I thank you.

PRESIDENT LOESEL: I am sure that we have all benefited by this fine address. I want to thank you, Dr. Carstens. I am glad we had the opportunity of hearing you.

The next on the program is "What Pennsylvania is Doing." The first speaker will be Mrs. Jackson S. Schultz, President of the Children's Aid Society of Western Pennsylvania.

WHAT WESTERN PENNSYLVANIA IS DOING

Mrs. Jackson S. Schultz

The field of Western Pennsylvania is a large one, and one in which there is abundant opportunity for service. In the cities and larger towns, industrial plants employ hundreds of foreigners; in numerous small communities, where the houses are clustered about a tannery, a chemical works, a brick plant, a pumping station, there are many underprivileged children. The smaller mining towns are forlorn places, and when the mines are working, conditions are none too good; when they are shut down, there is overwhelming need, which must be taken care of by county officials and by welfare organizations. A great number of these tiny settlements are so remote that it is practically impossible to reach them during the winter and early spring months.

Forty-one years ago, there were organized in Western Pennsylvania the first groups of workers to care for dependent and neglected children, and to assist the Directors of the Poor and the County Commissioners in finding homes for them, so that the crowded conditions of the County Homes might be relieved.   The movement grew, till in every county of the section there were societies of earnest and devoted women who, because of their love for children, gave of their best effort.   It was a decided step in advance, and resulted not only in removing children from the almshouses, but in keeping them from being sent there.   The groups, small at first, and working within a narrow radius, of which in most cases the county-seat was the center, have become larger; through county organization and greatly increased membership it has become possible to reach a much greater number of children, and to give them more adequate supervision.   Increasing knowledge of the needs of children has resulted in broadened activity; more effort is made to preserve the unity of the home when poverty threatens its disruption; much attention is given to the health of the children and to the correction of their physical defects, which so seriously handicap them; in counties where the Mothers Assistance Fund does not function, the relief given by Directors of the Poor is supplemented by the Children's Aid Society, so long as there may be need.   Assistance is given unmarried mothers to enable them to keep their babies whenever possible.

The Children's Aid Society is active in twenty-two counties of Western Pennsylvania, Westmoreland, Crawford, and Clinton Counties working independently, and having their own Children's Home.

In the year ending June first, 1927, there were admitted 599 children, which with those already in care, made a total of 1434 given care during the year.   Of those admitted, 66 were received from the Directors of the Poor, 60 from the Juvenile Court, and 7 from the almshouse.

122 mothers and 42 fathers were given assistance in caring for their children; there were admitted to hospitals and clinics for operations and for treatment, 196; there were placed in free homes for permanent care or for adoption 169; and 100 were placed in boarding homes.   164 were given supervision in their own homes; some of these children were supplied with milk, some with clothing — others were visited frequently during the time they were recovering from operations, to make certain that they were having proper care during that period.   At the close of the year, of the 851 in care 10 were colored children, and 110 were children under three years of age.   In Clearfield, Fayette, Mercer, McKean, Somerset, Venango, and Warren Counties are receiving homes, maintained by the Children's Aid Societies of those counties.   Children are placed there for temporary care, to give opportunity for the correction of physical defects, for observation and study, and for training, before they are sent to private homes. Their capacity ranges from twelve children in the Venango County C.A.S. Home, to fifty in the Warren County C.A.S. Home.

In addition to these homes, and those in Pittsburgh and Erie, there are in Western Pennsylvania eighteen homes for children, housing approximately a thousand children, many of whom are in those homes for permanent care. Some are. maintained by the county, some by religious or fraternal organizations, and a few are homes established by individuals and maintained by solicited subscriptions. Undoubtedly some of these little children are not normal children, but would not the majority of them be happier in private homes, as members of a family group?

Forty years ago, the Children's Aid Society was the only county agency working for children, and even now, in some of the counties, it is the only private agency giving care to the dependent child. The Juvenile Court deals with delinquents, and in five counties employs both man and woman probation officers; the Mothers Assistance Fund which functions in all except Forest, Elk, and Cameron Counties prevents separation of mother and children; the Anti-Tuberculosis Society, in addition to its other work, furnishes milk to children; the Red Cross, the Fraternal organizations, the Service Clubs, the Woman's Clubs, the Y.M. and the Y.W.C.A., the Boy and the Girl Scout movements — all are helping to add to the health and the well-being of the boys and the girls of today. Workers for these organizations and for various industrial concerns, are co-operative with the Children's Aid Society groups, making it possible, often, to do more effective planning for the children. Allegheny, Beaver, Butler, Erie, Fayette, Lawrence, Mercer, and Washington Counties lead in having trained social service for industrial concerns and for various agencies.

Allegheny, Erie, and Warren Counties have for several years had facilities for mental study of children, but other counties have not been so fortunate. Now, there are held weekly clinics in three counties, monthly clinics in twelve counties, and annual clinics in three counties. There is no longer an excuse for placement of children without having knowledge of their mental age.

We desire to acknowledge, with great appreciation, the co-operation of the Directors of the Poor and of the County Commissioners. Without their assistance, the efficiency of our work would be lessened.

The nature of the co-operation varies in the different counties. In one, a lump sum of five hundred dollars is given monthly to the Children's Aid Society of that County for the care of its children: in another, bills for clothing, for board, and for transportation of the children who are received by the Children's Aid Society from the Directors of the Poor, are cheerfully met. In some counties, the children taken in charge by county officials are not taken to the almshouses, but are given at once into the care of the Children's Aid Society, to be examined, clothed, boarded for a longer or a shorter period, and if placeable, to be finally placed in a family home. The rate of board paid is $5.00 weekly, in the majority of the counties.

The work of the Directors of the Poor and of the Children's Aid Society is closely related — both groups have responsibility for dependent children, and feel in duty-bound to supply to them so far as is possible, that of which they have been deprived, a home, understanding and loving parents, an education, religious training, and an opportunity for development along the line of their special aptitude.

It was a pleasure Monday Evening to hear your President stress the importance of thorough investigation. In no branch of your work is it more necessary than in the work for the dependent children of your Counties.

Time was, when it was well-nigh impossible to obtain from the Directors of the Poor, any family history of the children given to the care of the Children's Aid Society a name, and the clothes on their back were all that came with them. But standards of child care have changed, — We all recognize the importance of obtaining full information about the child, and his family; we know the need of study, both of the child and of the home to which he may be sent; and we realize the great need of frequent visiting and of intelligent supervision in our work.

But, investigation, study of the children and the homes, frequent visiting, the making of records of family history, and of developments from week to week require much time and much work. Are you, and are we, doing this work for children as thoroughly as it might be done? The underlying thought of this conference has been the desire to advance and to give the best possible service to the dependents of Pennsylvania. For four years, Beaver County has demonstrated the value of trained social service in that county.

It is quite possible that other counties would be interested in making a similar experiment, if it could be done without too great expense. Would it not be feasible for the Directors of the Poor to join with Children's Aid Society groups in making such an experiment for a year, each group meeting half the expense of the program? While in some of the Western Counties, there is a sentiment about having the work for children of the county done by citizens of the county, and a consequent opposition to trained social service, in others there is a desire for assistance of trained workers, and only the difficulty of financing such service has held them back.

It is my belief that the close of such an experiment would show results which would more than justify the added expenditure — that a more constructive work for both families and for dependent and neglected children would result.

The people of Western Pennsylvania are interested in the work for children — the interest is county wide, as is evidenced by the generous contributions, both to the Receiving Homes, and to the general work of the counties which have not such homes; this support will increase proportionately with the volume and efficiency of the work.

Shall we not take a step in advance this year by placing in the field of Western Pennsylvania, workers of training and of experience in family case work and in work for children? Shall we not plan to give less institutional care to normal children this year, and to place more children in carefully selected family homes? Only in such homes will the dependent children of our state develop into the type of citizens needed in our Commonwealth.

PRESIDENT LOESEL: The next will be a speech by Miss Abigail F. Brownell, County Agency Department, Children's Aid Society of Pennsylvania.

WHAT EASTERN PENNSYLVANIA IS DOING
Miss Abigail F. Brownell

You have heard both yesterday and this morning about cooperation and its importance in working with people who are clients of social agencies. I would like to tell of a cooperation that has been going on between the Directors of the Poor and the Children's Aid Society of Pennsylvania for the past 46 years, in caring for dependent children. In the last 20 years more than 1600 of the children received into the Main Office of the Children's Aid Society in Philadelphia came from the Directors of the Poor in 25 different counties in the eastern part of the state.

In 1921, when our family of 2200 children was rapidly growing larger and even so we were not beginning to meet the needs of dependent children in Eastern Pennsylvania, the County Agency Department was started to help counties organize to take care of their own children. It was felt that better care could be given to more children on this plan of a county unit, and that this could be done at less expense. Eastern Pennsylvania is a large territory to travel over to investigate applications for care for children. Since then the Directors of the Poor have been cooperating with us in the counties where we have agencies. The first six to be organized were Lycoming, and Bradford in 1922, Montgomery in 1923, Delaware, Berks and Northampton in 1924. Susquehanna and Lehigh Counties opened offices during the past summer. The Department started with the idea that each County Agency would have directing its work a committee of representative citizens from that county. This committee would be responsible for the employment of a trained social worker, who was approved by the County Agency Department and could take charge of the work with the children. Today we have from one to three case workers in each of the eight county agencies. Since no two of the counties are alike, and we have tried to develop plans to meet the individual needs of each county, the eight Agencies today are each fulfilling somewhat different functions. All of them are placing children in foster homes, some of them are making investigations for institutions in their own communities and some of them are caring for children in their own homes when there is no family agency to do this. On August 31st of this year we had 700 children in the care of these eight agencies, 210 of them in boarding homes, 150 in free homes, 255 in their own homes and 78 in institutions.

Our aim is to give understanding care to our children, (realizing that one man's meat is another man's poison), to try to know our children, how they became what they are and what they need for their development. We try to work out a plan for each child that will give that child what he needs. If the child must go to an institution, the superintendent can know him better and plan more wisely for him if he has been studied. After this careful study no child goes to an institution who does not need that kind of care. If he can stay with his own family he is left there. If he needs a foster home it is more nearly possible to select just the right one.

After six years of work we feel convinced that better care can be given on a county plan. Doubtless some of you have been annoyed because the Main Office has had to refuse to take into care children whom you have referred. We are offering, however, without charge, help to any county that wishes to organize to take care of its own children. We feel that there are certain definite advantages to a county in being part of a larger organization such as ours. In the first place, the Main Office has had 46 years of experience and has learned from its failures as well as from its successes. Since the County Agency Department keeps closely in touch with all the County Agencies, these agencies can have the benefit of each others experiences. The Main Office still offers care to children who need placement away from their own community, as for whom medical care cannot be secured in their own communities, and it makes available to the counties its own Child Study Department. Although the problem of securing well equipped personnel for County Agency jobs is far from easy, our experience is that social workers are more interested in taking positions in smaller communities when they can be part of a larger agency and keep in touch with the Main Office.

Although our plan changed in 1921, we are now offering more help to the dependent children of the eastern part of the state, · We believe that the same cooperation between the Directors of the Poor and our Society that has been in existence in the past will bring still better results in the future.

PRESIDENT LOESEL: Your Committee on Officers acted wisely in selecting Mr. Charles L. Huston as our new President. Mr. Huston is unable to be with us this evening, and at this time I wish to introduce our new President.

Mr. Huston has been on the Board of Chester County for a period of 20 years and is a practical business man. I take great pleasure in introducing Mr. Huston.

PRESIDENT-ELECT CHARLES L. HUSTON: Ladies and Gentlemen: I am very glad indeed to greet you in this capacity. I will do my best to serve the Association during this coming year. I will try and familiarize myself with the details of the work throughout the state, and trust that we put into practice some of the benefits derived from these splendid addresses.

I regret very much indeed that circumstances made it impossible for me to remain for the evening addresses and carry out the program which has been outlined. I had made arrangements to return to another part of the State and others are expecting me there. It is necessary that I leave this afternoon. I trust that you will have a splendid finish of the convention and take home with you a great deal of information that can be put into practice, for I am sure it is the best way in which to carry out this very important work which has been committed to our care. I thank you.

 ... Meeting adjourned at 11:50 o'clock ...

                                                    ADJOURNMENT

WEDNESDAY EVENING SESSION
October 5, 1927.

The meeting convened at 8:10 o'clock, President Charles F. Loesel presiding.

PRESIDENT LOESEL: The meeting will please come to order. The invocation will be made by Rev. Franklin T. Esterly, Pastor of Christ Evangelical Lutheran Church, Hazleton.

... Rev. Franklin T. Esterly made the invocation at this time ...

PRESIDENT LOESEL: The first number on our program this evening is "The Greatest Need of our State Institutions—a discussion of the Fifty Million Dollar Bond Issue," by Dr. H. Frazier, President of the Public Charities Association of Pennsylvania.

PENNSYLVANIA'S GREATEST PUBLIC NEED

Dr. Charles H. Frazier, Philadelphia

Every member of this audience knows that for years the development of our State institutions for the care and treatment of the insane, the feeble minded and epileptic and for the confinement and rehabilatation of offenders has not kept pace with the growing and recognized needs of these unfortunate classes. In consequence our great Commonwealth is inadequately equipped to perform one of its principal functions.

The people of Pennsylvania, through just such influential organizations as yours, must be made to face this situation squarely and decide whether or not the State shall be provided with the facilities necessary. Shall it be permitted to furnish efficient and scientific care to these, its helpless wards, and to maintain humane and constructive confinement of its offenders?

The only practicable way to meet this greatest public need of Pennsylvania is ratification by the people of the Bond Issue for the State's Unfortunates, passed by the last two legislatures. This Resolution would amend the Constitution so as to authorize the State to issue bonds not to exceed $50,000,000 to finance construction of state-owned institutions for the feeble-minded, epileptic and insane, penal offenders and delinquents. It is estimated that this sum will be adequate to take care of a ten-year building program.

Overcrowding

This general situation of the inadequacy of our State institutions and the proposed way to remedy the evil by a carefully earmarked Bond Issue, I believe you all know. But do you know that there are 2092 insane patients who cannot get proper care in our Pennsylvania hospitals today? Why not? Because there are not enough beds for them. 2592 other insane patients are on parole. Do you know that overcrowding is so great that many of these helpless patients are sleeping in dark hallways, on mattresses, on the floor, in places meant for sitting rooms? Do you know that during the last five years there has been an average increase of 1136 insane patients each year over the year before? Do you know that the American Legion reports 1200 Pennsylvania ex-service men as mentally ill and that 700 of these boys have to receive care outside of Pennsylvania because we have no room for them?

In the treatment of the insane it more than pays the state to do that work on the most efficient basis. The better the facilities for care and treatment, the more quickly patients can be cured or sufficiently improved to return to the community so that the state is relieved of the cost. Under present conditions of overcrowding, with inadequate facilities both for patients and staff, the state hospitals are greatly handicapped in their curative work. Apart from all questions of humanity, sympathy, pity or even of justice, the most humane and scientific treatment of the insane is the most economical for the state.

You see, we have gotten by the time when we look at the insane patient as incurable, and merely shut him up in an asylum. It used to be that when a person became insane, the only thought was to place him somewhere in order to protect the community. It was done for the safety of the community, and steps were taken at once to put the maniac into an asylum. Everybody then forgot about him.

Contributions have been made to the mental hygiene treatment, and now 20 per cent of those cases are curable, and a considerable number are preventable. The means and treatment for the care of the insane are just as effective as those applying to our sick people in other kinds of hospitals.

There is no doubt but what the improvement will more than justify the expense.

Moreover, there is to be considered the fact that without skillful treatment, mental disease may become chronic and render the patient dependent for the rest of his life. Furthermore there is to be considered not only the cost of supporting the patient, but the fact that the family which is left behind when the wage earner must go to the hospital may also become dependent upon public or private charity.

The restoration to a family of a father or mother or son or daughter under favorable hospital conditions, who under unfavorable conditions might become an incurable patient and require life-long care in a hospital, means a tremendous saving when considered merely in terms of cold cash.

How about the feeble-minded? In our three institutions for mental defectives there are now 1140 more than there is room for.

There is no economy in the postponement of our obligations. Our policy in regard to the feeble-minded is constantly rolling up a heavier bill. To take a few concrete instances:

Since 1913 four feeble minded daughters of a feeble minded mother have cost the city of Philadelphia $20,000, and as they are all under 25 years of age and in good health they will certainly cost the city at least $50,000 before they die.

In one Pennsylvania city a study was made recently which showed the results of the marriage of two feeble minded women with two low grade men. Among the descendants are feeble minded, epileptics, alcoholics, insane, persons sexually promiscuous, known to courts, etc., in all upwards of 100 individuals who are "cases" of the Family Welfare Society. Segregation of these two feeble-minded women some years ago would have presented this social wreckage.

There are over 1500 such cases now on the waiting lists of the three state institutions for the feeble minded. There are hundreds more in the care of local and private agencies, not intended for the care of this type of case, and in jails and penitentiaries. There are hundreds more at large. No one can compute the cost to the community of the neglect of this class. Have you ever tried to get a feeble minded person into one of our State institutions and found out how hard it is?

Ladies and Gentlemen, do you realize that in one of our state schools for the feeble minded there are now 975 inmates over capacity? The children sleep in double decked beds and in the school rooms, on mattresses on the floor in the hospital building. Such overcrowding curtails the training activities if the school and increases the difficulties of managment, but what is to be done?

Epileptics are even worse off. 1200 of these unfortunates are now mixed up with insane and feeble minded. They need a special institution for their care. The last Legislature made a small, initial appropriation to begin such as institution.

How about juvenile delinquents? Buildings are so overcrowded children have to sleep in double decked beds.

I don't suppose there is a week that goes by that I don't see a mother who brings in her child who manifestly is a mental defective, and is incurable. It is just as easy to make a feeble-minded child well as it is to grow another arm onto the child's body. And this mother has cherished the hope that this child might be restored to health. And then when the mother realizes that there is no hope for the child, the question is asked, "How am I going to get the child into an institution. The child must be taken care of".

And then when the proper authorities are interviewed, there is that long waiting list, and it may be two or more years before the child is admitted. The mother's health breaks down trying to care for the child, and as a result the family is demoralized.

Most of you are familiar with examples where a young boy or girl begins to show signs of epilepsy, and cases of convulsions. At first perhaps they are not bad, and only keep the child out of school for a period of time. They then become more frequent, and later the child must go to an institution. Where can we send children like that? Here are boys and girls whose mothers can't take care of them at home, and they are unable to secure employment. There are only two places where you can send boys and girls like that. You can send them to the feeble-minded institution, but they do not belong there because they are not feeble-minded. . They are normal children, but they are cursed with these occasional attacks. ;

If you don't send them there, where do you send them?   Insane asylum? It is tragic to send a child who is normal in every respect but those occasional attacks, to an institution where they are all insane.   It is a blow to the family to face a situation like that.

There will be an institution provided providing this Bond Issue is voted upon favorably in November 1928.

In the beginning of the 19th century Pennsylvania led the way in prison building but in this, the 20th century, our penitentiaries have become obsolete.   The Eastern Penitentiary (built in 1829) has 1624 men in cells built for 1100.

Staff Living Conditions Unbearable

Not only are our institutions seriously overcrowded but the living quarters of our medical staff, of the nurses and attendants are often so unsuitable that there is a constant and expensive labor turn-over.   For example, in some instances the dental hygienist and occupational therapists are crowded three in a room in the same quarters with the maids and kitchen help. Nurses are required, after a 12-hour day in an atmosphere that is far from normal and depressing in the extreme, to occupy rooms in the same wards, among the same patients with whom they have worked all day, and there attempt to sleep amidst the noise and confusion incident to the housing of mentally disturbed patients.

Do you wonder that our hospitals are not properly manned and vacancies exist on the medical staff and that it is almost impossible to induce a high type of young physician to engage in work of this character.

Curative Work Handicapped

The great object sought in the hospitalization of the mentally ill is obviously the scientific medical treatment with a view to curing the mentally diseased and restoring the individual to social and economic efficiency rather than to provide an asylum for him at the expense of the taxpayers. Without question the present situation of neglect is demoralizing to our ward employees and medical officers.   It is productive of much harm to our patients who are tending to become members of a group with a consequent loss of that individual treatment that is so essential to improvement and cure.   It is impossible to give the best chances of recovery to mentally disturbed patients when they are crowded together due to the conditions existing to day in our mental hospitals.

I was talking to one of the medical staff of a state institution the other day and found there were upwards of 3,000 patients in that institution. How many doctors do you suppose there were who took care of these people?   Only six!   How under the sun could the six doctors give those 3,000 patients the proper care?   Of course they were not all acute cases, but you can easily understand that a staff of that size is inadequate to properly manage and handle the situation.

Clinic Cases Neglected

The Department of Welfare has established 57 mental clinics through which pass day after day mentally defective boys and girls who cannot be properly cared for at home, for whom the only solution is a school for defectives. But many of the applications for admission to the state schools were filed several years ago and still there is not room. There are hundreds of women of child-bearing age who pass through these clinics but the State has made almost no provision for them. To these clinics, too, come people suffering from mild and curable cases of mental disease who may be admitted as voluntary patients to the State hospitals. At the present time, however, the State is not equipped to treat properly this type of case. A physician at one of our large State hospitals states, "There are few wards set aside for these early, mild and curable cases, and the patient if he comes for treatment may find his bed among the acutely disturbed homicidal or suicidal patients."

Yesterday in Pittsburgh, I saw a doctor who attended one of these mental clinics and he stated that in the course of a period of time, they had ear-marked 80 patients who were in need of institutional care, and after a vigorous campaign, trying to place these patients, they finally succeeded in getting in only two.

Fire Risks are Great

Early in 1923, 22 insane patients and 3 attendants were burned to death in a fire which destroyed one of the buildings of the Manhattan State Hospital for the mentally ill on Ward's Island, New York City. This building was built in 1870 before modern methods of fireproofing were known. **In Pennsylvania hundreds of helpless victims of mental disorders are crowded in equally inadequate buildings.**

Need of two new types of State Institutions

a. Institution for male defective delinquents.

These subnormal offenders, these feeble minded criminals, now form the bulk of the "repeaters" in our penal institutions. Many require indefinite custody.

b. Psychopathic Hospitals

If we are to do effective work in the **prevention** of mental diseases we need two state psychopathic hospitals, one in the eastern and one in the western part of the State. These are institutions for the study, observation and treatment of incipient and largely recoverable cases of mental disease and incidentally furnish the facilities for psychiatric training. Their great value as a factor in the prevention of mental disease has been recognized by most of the other important states of the Union. Not only for the training of nurses, but the training of physicians to take care of mental disease.

You must realize that there is just as much technique in the mental as in the practice of surgery. I would be just as unfit to step into a mental hospital as a mental doctor or a psychiatrist to handle any of our surgical problems.

We need in this State, as they put in other States, these so-called psychopathic hospitals, where they take the early mental disturbance patients and keep them under observation, as they use them in Boston, and as they are going to do in New York, for the training of these people. Some of you may have seen the magnificent institution that the state of New York is going to construct in New York City as a part of the program of Columbia University.

The average annual net increase of patients in the State and county hospitals means that every **two** years we need an additional hospital for the mentally diseased. The prospect would be profoundly discouraging if it were not for the fact that modern knowledge of mental hygiene holds out to us the hope that a considerable proportion of mental disease can be prevented. While it is the belief of psychiatrists that the most effective preventive work can be accomplished in childhood, it has been demonstrated that much incipient disease can be checked by prompt treatment of the adult.

With these facts in mind let us do more than deplore the inadequacy of our state institutions. We have a remedy at hand. And these are the facts as they exist in our State today, and you can help the movement forward if you are sympathetic at all by spreading the gospel far and wide. I assure you that I am not presenting these facts to stir up your emotions or bring tears to your eyes. These are just plain statements and are actual facts as they exist, and acknowledged to exist by those who know.

Our Legislatures of 1925 and 1927 have taken such action, which if ratified by the people next year will enable us to make provision for the development of these institutions to meet our needs. This opportunity will not knock at our door again for another five years.

We cannot afford to reject it. No other means of guaranteeing a continuous policy is practicable and we must establish a continuous policy if the building that the State has to do is to be done in a business-like way and in a reasonable amount of time.

There is no economy in the method we have had to pursue. Piece-meal construction is not only ineffectual but it is extravagant. Any one with any knowledge of building will admit that it costs infinitely more to build piece meal, it even results sometimes in the deterioration of the work under construction. To take one example – it took eleven years to build one of our finest State hospitals, that at Allentown. It could have been built in from two to three years. During eleven years the State invested money in this undertaking without getting any return. Not one patient was cared for. The interest on the State's investment of the first eight years at 4% would have amounted to about $400,000.

There is no economy in denying to our hospitals the developments they need to do their job efficiently.

As to the cost of the proposed bond issue two methods have been suggested. The total cost of one will be $62,000,000, of the other $71,000,000.

Let us assume, for the sake of argument, that we choose the more expensive of these two methods, which results in the lesser average annual burden, namely, $2,448,275. These would be 4% 20-year straight serial bonds, issued over a period of ten years. The average annual cost to the people of Pennsylvania would be 25½¢ per capita over a period of 29 years.

The cost of borrowing money will certainly be largely if not wholly offset by business like planning and letting of contracts, but it is certainly worth paying something to get what we need when we need it.

We believe that it is possible to take care of the annual charges of interest and retirement from our present current revenues **without additional taxation.**

As to the soundness of financing such capital developments from a bond issue, I do not believe there can be any question. The buildings which will be constructed from these funds will serve the State for a generation after the bonds have all been retired and forgotten. It is entirely equitable to spread the cost of such capital developments over a number of years. If, however, after the ratification of this amendment, the State should create a fund for capital developments, such as the Tax Commission has suggested, there is, of course, no obligation on the legislature to issue any more bonds than the situation demands.

There has existed an impression that business men do not look with favor upon this proposition. This measure has the support of many of the outstanding business men of Pennsylvania, such as General Harry C. Trexler of Allentown, Vice President of the Pennsylvania Manufacturers Association, Arthur W. Thompson, President of the United Gas Improvement Company, Thomas S. Gates of Drexel and Company, Ellis A. Gimbel, Samuel S. Fels and Albert M. Greenfield of Philadelphia, Alan Dodson of Dodson, Weston Co., Quincy Bent of the Bethlehem Steel Company and many others.

There is one more point that I wish to bring out. There has been criticism of this proposition from one quarter, based on the assumption that were this bond issue authorized there would follow an orgy of extravagance and corruption on the part of the Legislature. If such criticism ought to be taken seriously we might as well give up representative government entirely. In New York the expenditure of a similar sum was carefully and systematically planned with the advice of the best technical experts and it was put through by the Legislature with the upmost efficiency. No one has had one word of criticism of the way this money has been expended, not even Ogden Mills, and if he had nothing to say I expect the performance must have been flawless. I have never heard that New Yorkers were any more honest or any more efficient than Pennsylvanians. I think we can point with pride to the expenditure of twice this sum on our roads.

I believe the people will ratify this amendment. I believe that we can accomplish a vitally important task for the Commonwealth of Pennsylvania as a result of which we may look forward to a decrease in the burden of social wreckage which is now yearly growing heavier; as a result of which we will make Pennsylvania a leader in the handling of its social problems instead of a laggard as it is today. The administration by its support of this Bond Issue at the Legislative Session has inaugurated a new policy. Let us by our action guarantee popular approval in November 1928.

PRESIDENT LOESEL: Dr. Frazier is a very busy man. I understand that he was in Pittsburgh last night, and arrived here at Hazleton at 7:30 o'clock tonight. He has to leave again tonight, and I am sure that we all appreciate that he took the trouble to come here and make this fine address. We all know how essential it is to have larger and a greater number of institutions for the feeble-minded and mentally ill patients. I think we should all take a hand and try to pull across this Fifty-Million-Dollar Bond Issue.

The next will be an address by the Hon. Arthur H. James, Lieutenant Governor of Pennsylvania. He will speak to us on the subject, "The State and Local Community."

The STATE and LOCAL COMMUNITY
Hon. Arthur H. James

It is always a great pleasure for me to come to the "Beacon Light City" of the State of Pennsylvania. Some call Hazleton the "Mountain City," and when you stand off on the hillsides, you can regard it truly as the beacon light.

It is somewhat presumptuous on my part to come down here before this body of men and women and discuss a subject that might be of interest to you after listening to such a learned discussion. I just want to add a few words to what he has said to you in connection with my contact with some of the State institutions within the short time I have been charged with some of the responsibilities.

I can say to you that there is a great necessity of improvement in our State institutions and we ought to wholeheartedly support the proposition for an additional loan of $50,000,000.

The people of Pennsylvania ought to feel very proud on the question of bond issues. We are probably better situated financially than any other State in the Union. We have less bonded indebtedness than any other State. The money we have raised, particularly with reference to roads, I believe has been spent to better advantage than in any other State in the Union. So far as the use to which this money is going to be put, we have full faith that it is going to be properly expended.

I just wondered as I sat here tonight why they invited a Lieutenant Governor to address the body of the Poor Directors of the State of Pennsylvania. The fellow who personally invited me to come over here was John Bayless, and I think that John Bayless is perfectly aware of the fact that the chief function of the Lieutenant Governor is to be chairman of the Board of Pardons. Many of these responsibilities of the State, the Lieutenant Governor is not as familiar with as some of the other State officials.

You men and women are here to discuss a subject that is as old as the hills. There are two problems that people have always been confronted with—taxes, and the poor.

Taxation is a very vital question, particularly vital in many respects with reference to many of these new improvements that are being brought to our attention in so many different ways. And I want to digress a little, in speaking about constitutional amendments. It is very important to the people of the State of Pennsylvania that you have a Fifty-Million-Dollar Bond Issue for the miprovement of these buildings, these institutions. But we are going to have another constitutional amendment in the State of Pennsylvania just as essential, for the stability and integrity of the State of Pennsylvania—to see that we have voting machines in Pennsylvania which will eliminate considerable trouble.

I don't know whether you men and women throughout this great State of Pennsylvania have suffered as we have here in Luzerne County, but today, more than two weeks after the election, we finally discovered who was going to be one of our candidates for judge, and who was going to be our candidate for County Commissioner. And if that method is continned in Pennsylvania, or in any other country, it can't help but eventually mean the destruction of the institution we pride ourselves on. I say as an individual, and as a public official, that Pennsylvania ought to put the voting machine proposition over and it ought to put it over big.

As I said a few minutes ago, we have the taxes and the poor with us always. It has been the old story, and the one story that I think has been the most vital thing in every generation.

I can remember as perhaps the most pathetic thing of my childhood, of hearing of an old man or an old woman that went over the hills to the Poor House. And that question is just as acute today as it was then, and it is a problem that I just wonder sometimes whether, in the light of the progress that we have made in every other branch of governmental activity, we have given it the same degree of progress as you have given other things. For instance, the public schools, or the question of improved roads, or the health in the State.

You know there has been a great change as far as Pennsylvania is concerned with reference to the activities of the State and the local communities. If you and I were to go back 100 years we would find that the activities of the State were very, very much limited, largely to matters affecting the entire State. We had no such thing as public schools affecting Pennsylvania; we had no such things as public roads affecting Pennsylvania; and we had no such things as the Department of Health affecting Pennsylvania. And I doubt if we can find anything that affected the Poor, as far as Pennsylvania is concerned. It was solely a local proposition.

But with the advent of the new ideas, and "progress" as we call it, we are getting away from the idea that the local community can control its own affairs, and are now looking to the State, to the institution at Harrisburg, and look upon Pennsylvania as a great State. We are looking to Harrisburg to solve the problems of the State of Pennsylvania, as we look to Washington to solve the problems that affect this great country of ours.

Every time we want to settle a question today, we run down to Harrisburg and we introduce a new bill affecting that particular thing. As an illustration, if you were to go back 30 or 40 years ago, you would find that in State affairs the only thing that the State attempted to regulate was the medical profession and the legal profession. If you had been at the last session of the Legislature (and I see one or two members here tonight) you would find that instead of carrying out the general legislative programs that a Legislature did 25 years ago, its activities were largely focused upon taking care of some particular interest.

For instance, outside of the Appropriation Bill, and the Highway Bill, the activities of the members of the Senate and the members of the House were largely taken up by lobbyists who were supporting the Engineers' Bill, or the Barbers' Bill, the Brokers' Bill, etc. Each and every one of them are trying to regulate their particular line of business, or their particular profession, and they want Harrisburg to regulate that line.

We have in every sense of the word added practically every activity that the people of Pennsylvania can engage in by some form of legislation at Harrisburg. If you want to become an undertaker, you must go to Harrisburg. If you want to become an engineer, you must go to Harrisburg. And among these other Bills that are being introduced, you can hardly show a line of activity that you don't have to go to Harrisburg and get permission and consent to carry on your business. So, in a very large measure, you are losing sight of the local community. You are losing sight of the functions of the local community, of local government, and you are just simply turning all of your problems over and sending them down to Harrisburg for settlement.

That isn't the spirit of our American institutions. That isn't the spirit with which we founded a representative government. We are either all wrong in that respect, or we are going in this direction: that the people are not paying strict enough attention to the activities of the Legislature in matters which are affecting them individually and personally.

I say to you that in addition to that, who would think of a generation where we would have a Public Service Commission to regulate water and power companies. In every branch of the activities of the individual today in this community it is largely centered at Harrisburg, and the end is not here yet by a long ways.

Where does that problem bring you back to? It brings you back to this proposition: that the people have been more or less indifferent to this gradual encroachment by the State itself into matters and affairs very largely regarded as matters applicable to the communities themselves.

And you are soon going to call a halt to the situation, or the result will be that you will no longer have local community in the State of Pennsylvania, but you will have just one large legal entity located at Harrisburg.

I think it is wrong in principle to be compelling people throughout the State, to be diverting all of their interests to the point where every activity almost that you have, and go down to Harrisburg and take these matters up. I say this brings you to the other proposition that in the selection of representatives to the Legislature at Harrisburg, our people must be extremely careful to see that whatever steps are taken in the future to encroach upon those rights which have been always regarded as part of the local community's rights, that the local community's rights are protected.

It is a strange thing about Pennsylvania, although it is the greatest Republican State in the Union, and although Pennsylvania has always been trying to preserve the situation where the people will have the right to rule, we are finally getting to the point where the State is to be regarded as the sovereignty, rather than the local community. I think it is a step in which we are going just a little bit too far, and instead of having more centralization of power, we should have rather a decentralization of power in many respects and trust the people of particular communities with having some judgment and opinion in the matters.

I just wonder sometimes when you speak about the Poor whether or not you people have been going just as fast as you ought to go. When you speak about the Poor Board (and I must confess my unfamiliarity to a very large degree with the activities of the Poor Board as they have been extended during the past 15 or 20 years) I wonder if there has been any ultimate change whatsoever in the treatment of the Poor by the Poor Districts of Pennsylvania, from that of 300 years ago. Aren't you fundamentally in the same position—"Eventually they go to the Poor House?" And I don't know of any more pathetic thing in this world than the Poor House. It has stared every man and every woman for years, "Over the hills to the Poor House." And no matter what these other steps you may have taken, or perhaps modifying or softening, or making just a little bit easier, it is still, "Over the hills to the Poor House."

I say that is all wrong! And I don't know whether I am altogether in favor of the Old Age Pension Bill, but I am almost a convert.

A generation ago, yes less than that—fifteen years ago, the business interests of Pennsylvania said, "Let us not have a Compensation Bill because it will be confiscatory of the business of Pennsylvania." They thought it was going to cost too much money. You show me a business man in Pennsylvania today that will have the courage to get up in a public place and say that the Workman's Compensation Bill has been a mistake. They will say that it has been the most humanitary piece of legislation put on the books of our State in a generation. Where has their theory gone? It has been proven that it can be worked out successfully. Perhaps I wouldn't go so far as some of the advocates of the Old Age Pension Bill, but I think there is a happy medium for the solution to your problems, getting away from the "Over the hills to the Poor House." I think there is a happy medium where the hand of the law, through the instrumentality of the Poor Directors and the Poor Board can maintain that same indigent, that broken down man and woman; so that they may be able to live together in their declining years.

If we are going to consider this proposition on the basis of finances; as costing too much money, we might better stop where we are and not do anything at all; because if dollars and cents are going to stand in the way; and just merely take a nibble in trying to solve the problem, there is no use trying to solve the problem. Why not grasp it; just as Dr. Frazier said a few minutes ago—"Put the Fifty-Million-Dollar Bond Issue over because we need it."

That is the situation in Pennsylvania today. We are not properly solving the Poor problem, where indigent people in their declining years; through poverty and sickness and misfortune, are unable to take care of themselves.

Pennsylvania is too big a State, Pennsylvania is too rich a State to permit poverty in any sense to exist within its borders. We have more money, as far as a comparison of wealth is concerned, than any other State in the Union. There is no State in the Union that is more blessed by nature and by its peculiar geographical location than Pennsylvania. We have come to the front in almost every way.

In the days of 1776 Pennsylvania was the keystone of the 13 colonies. In the days of 1861 to 1865 we were the keystone of the Union. In the days of 1917 and 1918 we were important as an iron State, the Keystone State of the great armed forces of the World War. And it should never be said to the disgrace of Pennsylvania that she would not lend a helping hand to the utmost, no matter what the cost. In my opinion I don't think that cost alone is going to solve this problem, but I think that you Directors of the Poor can go to the people of this great State and say, "If it is a question of money, the people of Pennsylvania will vote and vote in a large majority for you."

I have talked just about 15 minutes longer than I had expected to talk. As I say, I don't know very much about the Poor problem, and I am glad that I have had the opportunity of saying a few words in an off-hand way regarding some of the opinions I have concerning your problem.

I am very glad to have had the opportunity of being with you. I thank you.

PRESIDENT LOESEL: I consider it an honor to have had the Lieutenant Governor present tonight. I have attended these conventions during the past 17 years and it is the first time that a Lieutenant Governor has spoken before our convention, I believe. We thank you very much for coming.

The next will be a report of the Solicitors' Round Table, and will be given by Mr. Harry A. Jones, of Washington County.

MR. HARRY A. JONES: Mr. President, Members of the Convention: Yesterday afternoon in one of the adjoining rooms was held a very interesting round table by the Solicitors and others interested in the legal problems connected with Poor relief.   There were 13 present, but notwithstanding that number, which is in disrepute, we held a very interesting and I think profitable meeting.   We continued to talk there and discuss the problems for something like two hours.

Naturally among a gathering of lawyers, the chief subject of discussion was "law", and there was discussed there the six pieces of legislation enacted at the recent session of the Legislature relating to Poor affairs.

For your own information (because the Pamphlet Laws have not yet been printed and distributed, owing to a fire in the State Printing Shop) may I briefly go over those several acts which were passed.

Acts Nos. 36, 43, 117, 265 and 490 affect amendments to various portions of the Poor Act of 1925.   Act No. 36 amends Sec. 907 thereof by including therein blind persons, including the right to arrange employment as well as a home for the subjects of the act, and permitting contracts to be entered into with employment associations for the purposes of the section.   The same act also amends Sec. 908 by including the blind and permits the Department of Welfare to place in the care of an association for poor relief subjects of the act who may not have been inmates of an Almshouse but otherwise entitled to relief.

Act No. 43 amends Sec. 200 of the act, by including the counties of Fulton and Cameron among the counties originally excluded from said provisions of the Act of 1925.

Act No. 117 amending Sec. 300 works what appears to be the most radical change.   It provides that in counties where, before the passage of the act, the county commissioners were Directors of the Poor they shall again so serve, and further that in counties which were created Poor Districts under the Act of 1925 the county commissioners shall be ex-officio Directors of the Poor.   This appears to wipe out automatically Directors of the Poor for districts which were created by the Act of 1925, and substituting in lieu thereof the county commissioners of the county, and re-instating as Poor Directors the county commissioners in counties where before the act county commissioners so served.   Under this act I should say that there would be no election for Directors at the coming election in counties covered by the section, and that Directors appointed or qualified under the Act of 1925 are automatically relieved from such duties.   This amendment is, in my opinion, subject to considerable interpretation as to exactly what it does mean, and I am therefore emphasizing it for your consideration.

Act No. 265 amending Sec. 1003 affects a radical change in the method of procedure enabling Poor Directors to take over the property of such persons who have become public charges.   The intention of the amendment unquestionably was to make such proceedings more formal, and require them to go through the channels of the proper court.   As I remember, there was considerable question whether or not the procedure as provided in the original section did not amount to the taking of property without due process of law, and was therefore unconstititional. You will note that it required merely an indexing or filing of a certificate of the action of the Directors. As amended it requires what amounts to a petition to the proper court with due notice and hearing. The only question that comes to me in examining the amendment is whether or not due notice as required by the amendment to be served upon the person should not also include some more specific provisions as to service on a minor, perhaps the appointment of a guardian ad litem, since I should imagine that service on a minor would constitute no service.

Act No. 490 amending Secs. 210 and 215 of said act, which sections refer to local Poor Districts, merely attempts to save the title of the property of county Poor Districts from any cloud which might be placed thereon by any interpretation of the sections.

Act No. 65 is a general regulation for all municipalities, including Poor Districts, and is intended to place the incurring of indebtedness of such districts under the supervision and control of the Department of Internal Affairs. The act speaks for itself.

PRESIDENT LOESEL: The next on the program is the report of the Committee on Legislation, to be given by Elmer E. Erb, Esq., of Harrisburg. Mr. Erb is not present and you will get this report in the completed report of the proceedings.

REPORT OF THE LEGISLATIVE COMMITTEE

To the President and members of the Association of Directors of the Poor and Charities and Corrections of the State of Pennsylvania:

We have the honor to transmit herewith the report of the Legislative Committee of this Association, in manner as follows:

We know that you are appreciative of the fact that matters of legislation are within the peculiar judgment and control of the Senators and Representatives chosen by the electors of this Commonwealth, and that furthermore, by concerted conference with and pressure and persuasion upon these members of the legislature on the part of their respective constituents, such as this great organization, the desired result can at times be obtained, or at least an accomplishment can be effected in furtherance of the cause.

At the same time, let us keep in mind that, out of this legislative body, comprised of human beings such as we who are assembled here tonight, possessed of varied personalities, dispositions, varied creeds, varied beliefs, varied social and business affiliations, and varied moral and intellectual calibre and standards, a majority or rather a two-thirds vote must at all times be obtained in order to effectuate the desired result.

During the session of the Legislature, sitting 1926-1927, a number of suggested laws pertaining to the poor and indigent were presented for legislation. Without commenting upon the wisdom of their becoming effective, or not becoming effective, we do report that some of them starved to death in the Committee — not this Committee — because, for peculiar and unexplained reasons, the Legislators sitting on this Committee did not see fit to give them sufficient nourishment so as to permit them to appear before the main legislative body, for their general inspection.

Some of these bills went gloriously through the House, and then died in the Senate; and some went through the Senate and faded into oblivion in the House.

Some of them actually survived the Committees, went through the first, second and third grilling and inspection of the House and Senate, and were then thrown over into the lap of our Governor, where they passed out, were buried, and were not given a tombstone or monument.

Some of them, gratifying to say, were nourished, bolstered and persistently pushed through Committee, House and Senate, and our good Governor christened them with his approval, thus placing them out upon our statute books.

Among the suggested laws which did not survive the Committee were the following:

House Bill No. 1915, by Mr. Dunn, presented March 28, 1927, providing for the appointment by certain cities, boroughs, incorporated towns and townships of persons to assist in the administration of the poor affairs there-' in, prescribing duties, etc.

House Bill No. 472, by Mr. Holcombe, February 2, 1927, amending Section 212 of the Act of 1925, P.L. 762 (the Poor Code) by providing additional compensation for County Treasurers in certain counties.

House Bill No. 443, by Mr. Holcombe, February 1, 1927, amending · Section 300 of the Act of 1925, P.L. 762 (the Poor Code), designating the County Commissioners as Directors of the Poor in eighth class counties. This bill took on an attack of paralysis in Committee, but later, strange to say, took new life in House Bill No. 448, again introduced by Mr. Holcombe, whereupon it actually passed the gauntlet in both houses. It appears, however, that this bill thereupon rested in the hands of the Governor.

House Bill No. 1187, by Mr. Baker, February 28, 1927, fixing salaries of Directors of the Poor in counties of the eighth class — died in the second round, before the House, March 14, 1927.

House Bill No. 1252, by Mr. McCormick, March 1, 1927, fixing salaries of County Poor Directors and Directors of Homes for the destitute in counties of the 3rd, 4th, 5th, 6th, 7th, and 8th, classes. This bill did not survive its first breath.

Senate Bill No. 1047, by Mr. Boyd, March 23, 1927, fixing the salaries of County Commissioners, for acting as such and as Directors of the Poor in counties of the 7th and 8th classes. After passing second reading in the Senate, it was re-committed to Committee on New Counties, etc., and there it died.

The following Bills died either in the House or in the Senate:

House Bill No. 1237, by Mr. Hubler, March 1, 1927; supplementing Act of 1874, P.L. 73, by providing that certain corporations may act as treasurers and tax collectors for Poor Districts.

House Bill No. 370, by Mr. Davies, February 1, 1927, providing that territory annexed to any city of the second class shall constitute a part of the Poor District of such city, or of the Poor District of which said city is a part.

Senate Bill No. 1047, by Mr. Boyd, March 23, 1927, fixing the salaries of County Commissioners for acting as such and as Directors of the Poor in counties of the 7th and 8th classes, that is to say $1300 in counties of the 7th class and $2000 in counties of the 8th class. This bill succumbed after the second round in the Senate.

House Bill No. 1187, by Mr. Baker, February 23, 1927, fixing the salaries of Directors of the Poor in counties of the 8th class at $400, but where acting also as County Commissioners, $200 additional. This bill went no further than second reading.

The following are the bills which died after passing through both House and Senate:

House Bill No. 1316, by Mr. Royle, March 2, 1927, amending Section 2, Act of 1807, P.L. 259, changing the corporate name of the District of Oxford and Lower Dublin in the County of Philadelphia, and providing for the purchase * * * * and sale of property, and the use of the proceeds acquired from sales and conveyance.

House Bill No. 1397, by Mr. Edward Brown, March 8, 1927, providing a Pension Fund for employees of District, City and County Homes and Hospitals for Mental Diseases. This bill went to Committee March 8, where it lay, an apparently unwelcome infant, until March 22, when someone generously lifted it out of its cradle and carried it before the House, where it was given such quick recognition that on March 30 it passed the House on final hearing.

Thereupon it went to the Senate, and on April 6th the Senate amended it slightly, and passed it on third and final hearing April 11, 1927. On April 12th, the House concurred in the amendment, whereupon it was delivered to the Governor. Unfortunately it died.

A similar bill went into the Senate March 7, 1927, Senate Bill No. 715, introduced by Mr. Sordoni. This bill passed the House by a vote of 46 to 0 and was thereupon given a rapid fire recognition by the Senate by a vote of 190 to 6.

This is the bill which received the unanimous support of the Executive Committee of this Association. Let it also be impressed upon you that this bill was drafted similarly to that of a bill pertaining to employees, etc., in third class cities, which actually passed both houses and was given the approval of the Governor.

We regret to report, however, that the Governor has vetoed this bill pertaining to pensions for employees of Districts, City and County Homes and Hospitals for Mental Diseases, etc.

House Bill No. 746, by Ella C. Adams, February 9, 1927, repealing Secttion 8 of the Act of June 13, 1836, P.L. 539, entitled "An Act Relating to the Support and Employment of the Poor, and Authorizing Overseers of the Poor to put out Children as Apprentices", reported to have rested in the hands of the Governor.

House Bill No. 1893, by Mr. McBride, March.28, 1927, amending Act of May 25th, 1883, "An Act to Provide for the Maintenance, Care and Treatment of the Indigent Insane in County and Local Institutions", as amended: increasing the weekly payments for each charge from $2 to $3 per week, and extending the provisions of said Act to Poor Districts, who supply, erect and maintain a suitable institution for the care and treatment of indigent insane.

This bill left Committee on April 4, 1927, and on April 12th it had already passed through both houses and into the hands of the Governor, where it is reported to have rested.

House Bill No. 448, by Mr. Holcombe, February 1, 1927, amending Section 300 of the Act of 1925, P.L. 762, here in above reported.

Senate Bill No. 72, by Mr. Schantz, January 24, 1927, fixing the salary of Directors of the Poor in Poor Districts of the 3rd and 4th classes, where such Directors are not also County Commissioners: that is to say $1500 in 3rd class districts, and $750 in 4th class districts. This bill passed both houses, and is reported to have rested in the hands of the Governor.

House Bill No. 1145, by Mr. Memolo, February 23, 1927, amending Section 18 of the Act of 1868 P.L. 660, entitled "An Act Authorizing the Erection of a Poor House by the Townships of North Abington, South Abington and Newton, Luzerne County". This bill passed both houses, and is reported to have rested in the hands of the Governor.

House Bill No. 1755, by Mr. Root, March 22, 1927, requiring public almshouses, hospitals, homes and institutions to keep on file and to forward to the State Department of Welfare a copy of the record of each honorably discharged soldier and sailor admitted thereto. This bill passed both houses, and is reported to have rested in the hands of the Governor.

The bills which passed both houses and which were approved by the Governor are as follows:

House Bill No. 925, by Mr. Goodnough, February 15, 1927, amending Sections 200 and 202 of the Act of 1925, P.L. 762 (the Poor Code), by exempting the Counties of Fulton and Cameron from the provisions of the Act. This act appears to be a step backward from the County Unit Plan in that the above counties may now maintain management under the plan which existed previous to the enactment of the Code. However, this bill passed both House and Senate, and was actually given the approval of the Governor.

Senate Bill No. 466, by Mr. Weingartner, amending the Act of 1925 P.L. 762 (the Poor Code), constituting the County Commissioners in certain districts as Directors of the Poor. This bill passed both House and Senate, by a vote of 46 to 0 in the former and by 197 to 0 in the latter, was approved by the Governor, and is also now a law.

Senate Bill No. 198, by Mr. Lanius, February 7, 1927, amending Sections 907, 908, of the Act of 1925 P.L. 762, (the Poor Code), providing for the relief and care of the Blind. This bill passed both houses without a nay, and was approved by our good Governor within one week from its final passage. The previous laws made no provision for the Blind. We feel that through the faithful activities of Mrs. Mary Dranga Campbell, Executive Director, State Council for the Blind, a great influence was exerted toward the enactment of this helpful legislation.

House Bill No. 443, by Mr. Holcomb, Feburary 1, 1927, amending Section 300 of the Act of 1925, P.L. 762, providing for continuance as Directors of the Poor of County Commissioners, who were Directors of the Poor, previous to the Act of 1925; and providing further that, where County Poor Districts were first created under said Act, as County Poor Districts, the County Commissioners shall be ex officio Directors of the Poor. This bill passed both houses, was approved by the Governor, and became a law.

Senate Bill No. 387, by Mr. Baldwin, February 15, 1927, providing for the supervision by the Department of the Interior Affairs over matters pertaining to the increase of indebtedness of *** Poor Districts,r equiring reports to be made, etc. This bill having passed both houses, and having received the approval of the Governor, became a law.

House Bill No. 1202, by Mr. Hantz, March 1, 1927, amending Sections 210 and 215, of the Act of 1925, P.L. 762, (the Poor Code), by defining the legislative intent as to the vesting of the title to property of County Poor Districts, holding that nothing in this section shall apply to the property of any County Poor District in whom the property shall vest and be controlled by the Directors of the Poor of such County Poor District. This bill passed both houses, was given the final approval by the Governor and also became a law.

Senate Bill No. 464, by Mr. Weingartner, February 21, 1927, amending Section 211 and 212 of Article II, Chapter 2, and Section 1003 of Chapter 10, of the Act of 1925, P.L. 762 (the Poor Code).

The amendent to the aforesaid Section 211 supplanted the words "serve for a term not exceeding four years" for the words "one year"; and the amendment to Section 212 aforesaid, after authority given the Treasurer of the County to pay out money on the warrants of the Poor Directors, added the words "upon approval thereof by the County Controller".

Through an examination of the legislative records, it appears that these two portions of the Bill as thus introduced, to wit Sections 211 and 212, were lost by the legislature, and like the farmer who, having lost a goodly portion of his load of hay, proceeded onward with the rest of his load, the legislature went on with the rest of this load and enacted the aforesaid Section 1003.

It is to be recalled that, from the reports as given to this Convention out of the Solicitors Round Table Conference of last year, there was some doubt as to the constitutionality of thes section as originally set forth in the Poor Code, for the reason that there appeared to have been no provision for the charge or the pauper to have his day in Court.

This act of 1927, as now approved by the Governor, requires the presentation by the Directors of the Poor to the Court of Common Pleas, where such charge is of full age, or to the Orphans Court, where such charge is a minor, for a citation upon such person to show cause why the said Directors shall not become the legal custodians of all the property, real, personal and mixed, of such public charge. In connection with this petition the Act furthers requires the attachment of an inventory of all of the Property belonging to such charge, together with a statement setting forth that such person is a public charge upon the Directors.

Thereupon the Court shall fix a day when the matters concerning the charge shall be determined, but due notice is required to be served upon the person alleged to be a charge—thus giving him an opportunity to be heard in Court.

Upon the day set for hearing, the Court may, after determining the fact, make an order constituting the Directors of the Poor guardians of the person and estate of such charge. Thereupon, the matter is indexed upon the proper Court records and is notice to all of the world that the assets of such pauper are therefore in the control of the Directors.

This appears to be a very helpful and expeditious instrument, which serves as a protection to the alleged charge and aids the Poor District to a quicker access to the property of such pauper for his maintenance under them.

Another very important enactment is the one which was introduced by Mr. Sterling, January 31, 1927, to wit House Bill No. 276, which is the popularly discussed Joint Resolution pertaining to the fifty million dollar bond issue for the purchase of lands and buildings for the care of penal offenders and mental defectives.

This bill passed both of the houses and received the approval of the Governor. We believe it to be a most important piece of legislation; and the matter of its final determination will be left to the electors of this Commonwealth in the near future.

This Committee suggests to the members of this organization that, whenever any individual, or groups of individuals are desirous of having the enactment of certain laws, they put forth every effort to first impress upon their local representatives the details and importance of such legislation; and that they furthermore maintain a continuous watch upon the acts of their representatives, until something has actually been accomplished; or, in the event that such representatives or representative do not see fit to sponsor the suggested bill, to seek one who will take an active part and will continue until the end is accomplished or the obstacle is met.

The Committee suggests further that the members or persons desiring new legislation arouse the interest and activity of their friends and acquaintances, by urging them to confer with and write to their own representatives in the Legislature, as well as to as many of the legislators as they can possibly influence or persuade toward the enactment of the desired law. We cannot too thoroughly impress upon you the importance of persistent and detailed pressure on your part upon the representatives of your own communities, as well as upon every other representative who might be connected up with some personal friend or acquaintance of yours in the Legislature.

We desire to thank the various persons in our organization for their helpful suggestions and their kind co-operation in the matter of obtaining the few results which were obtained for us in the recent sittings of the Legislature.

Respectfully submitted,

ELMER E. ERB, *Chairman*

C. W. SMILES.

HARRY A. JONES.

F. KENNETH MOORE

PRESIDENT LOESEL: The next will be the report of the Committee on Resolutions. Mrs. E. C. Dunn is Chairman of that committee, and I will ask her to make her report at this time.

MRS. E. C. DUNN: Mr. Chairman, Directors of the Poor, Superintendents, Matrons, and Friends: The Committee on Resolutions desires to make its report and offers the following resolutions for adoption:

Resolution No. 1.

"WHEREAS, the City of Hazleton, with its various civic organizations and the Middle Coal Field Poor District, with its officers as hosts at this 52nd Annual Convention of the Association of the Directors of the Poor and Charities and Corrections of Pennsylvania have gone the limit in making every one feel at home, stamping this as one of the most successful affairs in the history of the Association; therefore be it

"RESOLVED, that the Convention expresses its sincere thanks for the warm reception and hospitality enjoyed by every member present. The appreciation of the Convention is also extended to the local Chamber of Commerce, Mr. and Mrs. G. Stewart Engle for the wonderful entertainment furnished the ladies and to the local newspapers for their contribution along the lines of publicity, they have been most generous in giving space to our proceedings and the accounts form a complete accurate synopsis for the convention proceedings that will prove of invaluable service to our delegates on their return to their homes; and therefore be it further

"RESOLVED, that the Convention voices its most heartfelt gratefulness to the congregation of St. Paul's Methodist Church for the housing of the convention during deliberations; and lastly be it

"RESOLVED, that appreciation be extended to the speakers, as well as to all the officers of the Association who were instrumental in making this occasion a memorable one."

Resolution No. 2.

"WHEREAS, it has pleased God in His eternal wisdom to remove Mr. H. Wilson Stahlnecker, Mr. Frank Bausman, and Mr. H. H. Pensyl from our midst; and

"WHEREAS, they were faithful public servants in their respective communities, as well as in the ranks of our Association; therefore be it

"RESOLVED, that the Association expresses its deep sorrow for the loss of these members, and extends its sincere condolence to their families by sending a copy of this resolution to them."

Resolution No. 3.

"BE IT RESOLVED, that in debating any question before the convention a person shall be limited to a period of five minutes unless permitted by the Chair to speak longer."

Resolution No. 4.

"RESOLVED, that every Poor District adopt the system of a Social Service Exchange."

Resolution No. 5.

"RESOLVED, that the Association is in full accord with the joint resolution passed by the last two sessions of the Legislature for the issuance of a $50,000,000 loan for the construction of State institutions for the insane, feeble-minded, epileptics and delinquents, and the Association gives this resolution its unqualified endorsement."

Resolution No. 6.

"WHEREAS, two sessions of our Legislature have passed a bill sponsored by this Association for creating a pension or retirement fund for employees of District Mental Hospitals and District and County Homes, each time vetoed by our Governor; and

"WHEREAS, at the last session an act similar in every particular applicable to employees of Third Class Cities not already protected was passed and signed; and

"WHEREAS, this Association is still in favor of having such bill enacted; therefore be it

"RESOLVED, that this Association go on record as being strongly in favor of such bill."

Resolution No. 7.

"WHEREAS, the Convention learned of the resignation of Mr. Edwin D. Solenberger as Secretary, and of Mr. W. G. Theurer as Treasurer; and

"WHEREAS, these officers were faithful servants to the Association for the past twelve years, during which period both of them gave their time, knowledge, experience and their untiring effort that the Association might develop into what it is today; therefore be it

'RESOLVED, that the Association regrets most profoundly the steps taken by said officers and considers their resignation a distinct loss; and be it further

"RESOLVED, that the Convention extend a vote of thanks and appreciation to the said officers for their efficient and honorable work within the Association.   The Convention feels that it was through their prudent guidance that the Association was able to continue its noble work.   Their absence will be keenly felt and if the Association will go forward in spite of their absence it will be because they showed the way."

**

... Mrs. Dunn spoke as follows concerning resolution No. 5:

How dare we say that we cannot afford that $50,000,000 loan?   Does not each and every woman Director here know that it is absolutely necessary that we have some place to put our women and our men?   Do you realize in our own county of Montgomery (and we are very proud of our County Home) instead of the County Home being a home of dear old fathers and mothers, such as it is meant to be, it is but a melting pot for every disease under the sun.

We have one woman, a young woman, in our home who is the mother (as near as we can get the history of her) of seven illegitimate children, and there is no reason that she may not be the mother of eight or ten. Our nurses can't watch these women.

Have the taxpayers of Pennsylvania the right to say to us Directors of the Poor that we shall not have that loan when we know there is an absolute necessity of having such a loan?   Is that what we Directors are for, to watch such women?

... Mr. Solenberger was presented with a handsome Gladstone traveling bag at this time ...

SECRETARY SOLENBERGER: Madam, Chairman of the Committee on Resolutions, Lieutenant Governor, Ladies and Gentlemen: In all of my experience I do not know that I have ever before known the committee on resolutions to present anything so concrete and definite as this beautiful gift. I wish to assure Mrs. Dunn that it was most unexpected at this moment.

I find it difficult to find words to adequately express to the Convention my thanks for your grateful kindness. I assure you that I appreciate it, and shall treasure this gift from you as the evidence of your continued loyalty to the work for which this organization was started. I hope I shall not be absent next year, Mrs. Dunn. We are neighbors. I hope to come and shall have the chance, for the first time in 12 years, to sit down in the audience, realizing that it is my part to listen and let some one else carry the responsibility of seeing that the speakers are here on time.

I do want to thank again all of those who have expressed themselves through the Resolutions and those who have taken part in this beautiful gift.

PRESIDENT LOESEL: Mr. Solenberger, I am sure that I heard Mr. White say that you should open it, or shouldn't drop it. I think it is up to you to open it.

SECRETARY SOLENBERGER: Is it safe to open it in the presence of a State official? You make a speech, Mr. President, while I open it.

PRESIDENT LOESEL: As Mr. Huston had to leave this afternoon he will not appear on the program as stated.

According to the program I am supposed to say something. You have heard and have seen me all week and I certainly appreciate the number that have attended this Convention. The attendance is getting better each year, and more people are taking interest, even if they are unable to attend these annual meetings.

I wish to state that I have had fine cooperation from the Executive Board, and I appreciate it very much. I wish also to thank those who have spoken to us, as well as the officers who have taken part in this Convention.

I also want to thank Mr. E. J. McKernan and the members of the local committee for the hospitality they have shown us while here in Hazleton. They certainly received us with open arms. They have taken a great interest in this organization in trying to make it pleasant for us.

I don't want to take up your time, nor do I want you to feel as the colored man felt when the judge sentenced him to two years at hard labor.

One day the judge was handing out sentences, and a colored fellow was brought before him. The judge said to him, "Mr. Johnson, have you anything to say before the court?"

"No sah, no sah, Ise got nothin' to say."

The judge said, "All right, sheriff, take him away." And the sheriff started off with the colored fellow.

As they were going out of the room, the judge noticed that the colored fellow was saying something to the sheriff. He called to them, and said, "Sheriff, bring the prisoner back again."

The sheriff brought the colored fellow before the judge again, and the judge said, "Have you anything to say, Mr. Johnson, before the court now?

"No sah, jege, Ise got nothin' to say."

"What did you say to the sheriff a few minutes ago?"

"I jest sez, 'Dat jege am awful lib'ral with other people's time'."

I just want to thank you all again, and remain "yours truly."

SECRETARY SOLENBERGER: This fine toilet set was inside of the bag. I will have to make another speech. This indeed is a gift in itself. You are very generous, and I can only say again that you have pledged me for 12 years more, to labor in the ranks. If you will give Mr. Huston, Harry Jones and Dennis Mackin the same fine support you have given the outgoing officers, and will all work together, I am sure we can carry out and fulfill the objectives that Lieutenant Governor James has referred to. I thank you.

PRESIDENT LOESEL: This finishes our program, and this brings the 52nd Annual Convention to a close.

... The Fifty-Second Meeting of the Association of Directors of the Poor and Charities and Corrections of the State of Pennsylvania adjourned at 9:30 o'clock ...

ADJOURNMENT

ENROLLMENT OF DELEGATES

Hazleton, Pa., October 3–5, 1927.

ALLEGHENY COUNTY

Mrs. M. L. Zahniser, 207 Park Road, Rosslyn Heights, Carnegie.
Dr. G. A. McCracken, Woodville.
W. L. Henderson, East McKeesport.
Mrs. W. L. Henderson, East McKeesport.
H. H. Dixon, Millvale.
Major J. Clyde Miller, Homestead.
Andrew Zeok, 410 Avon Avenue, South Hills Station, Pittsburgh.

BEAVER COUNTY

Mrs. Esther Martin Sorg, Court House, Beaver.
Miss S. E. Springer, R. F. D. 1, Monaca, Beaver.

BEDFORD COUNTY

S. F. Campbell, New Enterprise, Bedford.
C. O. Brumbaugh, New Enterprise, Bedford.
J. Pearson Diehl, Bedford.
Mrs. J. Pearson Diehl, Bedford.
G. A. Hillegass, Buffalo Mills, Bedford.

BERKS COUNTY

A. B. Gerhardt, Wernersville, Reading.
A. F. Kramer, Shillington.
W. L. Snyder, Shillington.

BLAIR COUNTY

Carl G. Bridenbaugh, Hollidaysburg.
Mrs. Carl Bridenbaugh, Hollidaysburg.
Mrs. P. H. Bridenbaugh, Martinsburg.
P. H. Bridenbaugh, Martinsburg.
W. C. Bassler, 540 Maple Street, Roaring Spring.
Mrs. W. C. Bassler, 540 Maple Street, Roaring Spring.

BRADFORD COUNTY

Howard Bailey, Troy.
Mrs. Howard Bailey, Troy.

BUCKS COUNTY

Mrs. B. Fitzgerald, 510 Juniper St., Quakertown.
B. Fitzgerald, 510 Juniper St., Quakertown.
A. S. Kriebel, Doylestown.
Mrs. A. S. Kriebel, Doylestown.
Mrs. Hannah R. Leattor, 39 West State, Doylestown.

BUTLER COUNTY

J. T. Bricker, Butler.
Mrs. J. T. Bricker, Butler.

CAMBRIA COUNTY

Mrs. Alice Llewellyn, 263 Cypress Ave., Johnstown.
D. L. Owens, Ebensburg.
Mrs. D. L. Owens, Ebensburg.

CARBON COUNTY

Middle Coal Field District:
  (See Luzerne County)

CENTER COUNTY

David Vaughn, Sandy Ridge.

CHESTER COUNTY

Charles L. Huston, 64 S. First Ave., Coatesville.
Mrs. Charles Pyle, Kennett Square, Chester.
Mrs. Florence B. Cloud, Kennett Square, Chester.
W. B. Passmore, Embreeville, Chester.

CLEARFIELD COUNTY

T. R. Weimer, DuBois.
Jesse E. Dale, Clearfield.

CRAWFORD COUNTY

J. C. Boyd, Saegertown.
Mrs. J. C. Boyd, Saegertown.
H. S. Miller, 356 Rose Lane, Meadville.

CUMBERLAND COUNTY

George E. Reed, Carlisle.
W. D. Spangler, Newville.
J. S. Bitner, Enola.
H. A. Heberlig, Newville.
C. A. Shambaugh, Carlisle.
F. F. Lindsay, Carlisle.

DAUPHIN COUNTY

Mrs. E. S. H. McCauley, Claster Bldg., Harrisburg.
James C. Tucker, 3001 N. 3d St., Harrisburg.
Robert Helms, Claster Bldg., Harrisburg.
H. V. Sherman, Claster Bldg., Harrisburg.
Miss Isabel F. Pelly, Claster Bldg., Harrisburg.
Mrs. Mary Dranga Campbell, Harrisburg, Dept. of Welfare.
Albert B. Smith, 2050 Market St., Harrisburg.
Elmer E. Erb, Bergner Bldg., Harrisburg.
Mrs. Elmer Erb, Bergner Bldg., Harrisburg.
Mrs. R. B. Shunk, Room 6 Court House, Harrisburg.
Dr. John H. Lehr, 2533 N. Second St., Harrisburg.
Mrs. John H. Lehr, 2533 N. Second St., Harrisburg.
Mrs. C. C. Etnoyer, R. D. 1, Harrisburg.

DELAWARE COUNTY

Fred J. Siebrecht, Lansdowne.
Edwin D. Solenberger, 43 Brandon Road, Upper Darby.
Samuel G. Boland, Lansdowne.
Mrs. Fred J. Siebrecht, Lansdowne.

ELK COUNTY

Mrs. Jackson A. Schultz, 344 South St., Ridgway.

ERIE COUNTY

Dr. J. K. Tannehill, Girard.
H. E. Wagner, 3204 Buffalo Rd., Wesleyville.
Mrs. H. E. Wagner, 3204 Buffalo Rd., Wesleyville.
Chas. F. Loesel, 615 Poplar St., Erie.
Mrs. Chas. F. Loesel, 615 Poplar St., Erie.
Harriet M. Powell, 708 French St., Erie.
Mrs. R. E. Findley, Girard.
Homer A. Mills, East Springfield.
R. E. Findley, Girard.
Joseph Findley, Girard.

FAYETTE COUNTY

Frank Costolo, 702 Main St., Point Marion.
Geo. H. Krepps, E. Millsboro.
T. Springer Todd, Uniontown.
C. F King, R. D., Scottdale.
Mrs. Chas. P. Chick, 45 Morgantown St., Uniontown.
Mrs. Chas. King, R. D., Scottdale.

FRANKLIN COUNTY

Ira B. Wenger, Chambersburg.
Mrs. Lydia B. Wenger, Chambersburg.
Dr. W. E. Holland, Fayetteville.
John B. Stoner, Waynesboro.
P. H. Hollar, Chambersburg.

GREENE COUNTY

John L. Wood, 37 N. Richards St., Waynesburg
Mrs. J. L. Wood, Waynesburg.
Joseph Sproat, R. D., Waynesburg.
Mrs. Joseph Sproat, R. D., Waynesburg.
D. M. Thompson, R. D. 2, Waynesburg.
Grace Former, R. D. 1, Waynesburg.
H. H. Hughes, Waynesburg.
Mrs. H. H. Hughes, Waynesburg.

HUNTINGDON COUNTY

J. G. Allison, Mill Greek.
J. A. Price, Mount Union.
J. Q. Dell. Mapleton Depot.

INDIANA COUNTY

JUNIATA COUNTY

S. B. Hetrick, Court House, Mifflintown.
E. M. Nipple, Walnut.
J. H. Book, Mifflintown.

LACKAWANNA COUNTY

Scranton Poor District:

Thos. F. Wells, Brooks Bldg., Scranton.
M. J. McHugh, 1518 Luzerne St., Scranton.
Mrs. Millicent W. Harris, 813 Bromley St., Scranton.
Mary Murphy, 130 Dudley St., Dunmore.
Williard Matthews, Quincy St., Scranton.
Dr. Thomas A. Rutherford, Clarks Summit.
Mrs. T. A. Rutherford, Clarks Summit.
Wm. Koch, Jr., 723 Cedar Ave., Scranton.
John McNulty, 1690 Church Ave., Scranton.

Blakely District:

Thomas Grier, Main St., Dixon City.
R. J. Reese, 710 Pleasant Ave., Peckville.
Mrs. Wm. Watkins, Susquehanna St., Olyphant.
H. A. Thomas, R. F. D., Olyphant.

Carbondale District:

Mark Toolan, N. Main St., Carbondale.
Mrs. Margaret Brennan, 18 Sixth Ave., Carbondale.
John Connor, 67 Powderly St., Carbondale.
James Clark, R. D., Carbondale.

LANCASTER COUNTY

Mrs. W. C. Marshall, 132 E. King St., Lancaster.
Rev. P. L. Carpenter, Bird-in-Hand.
Samuel H. Boyd, 45 S. Fifth St., Columbia.
W. H. Bitner, 635 W. Chestnut St., Lancaster.
H. Walter Jones, R. F. D. 1, Christiana.
Wm. R. Good, R. D. 3, New Holland.
Hon. A. G. Seyfert, Lancaster.

LAWRENCE COUNTY

F. M. Davis, Wampum.

LEBANON COUNTY

A. G. Boger, Route 5, Lebanon.
Mrs. A. G. Boger, Route 5, Lebanon.
Wm. B. Shirk, R. D. 3, Myerstown.
John H. Swanger, 125 N. Sixth St., Lebanon.
C. T. Hickernell, 773 Cumberland St., Lebanon.
Mrs. C. T. Hickernell, Lebanon.
Mrs. Wm. B. Shirk, Myerstown.
Mrs. U. B. Siegrist, 425 Chestnut St., Lebanon.

LEHIGH COUNTY

Wm. H. F. Kuhns, Wescosville.
A. P. Roth, Allentown.
W. P. Deibert, 1343 Chew St., Allentown.
J. F. Beitler, Route 5, Allentown.

LUZERNE COUNTY

Middle Coal Field District:

Dr. J. E. Waaser, E. Mauch Chunk, Carbon County.
Mrs. J. E. Waaser, E. Mauch Chunk.
John T. Scanlon, Weatherly.
Mrs. Margaret Scanlon, Weatherly.
S. W. Drasher, Madison Ave., West Hazleton.
Mrs. S. W. Drasher, Madison Ave., West Hazleton.
John A. Bayless, Markle Bank Bldg., Hazleton.
Mrs. John A. Bayless, 436 E. Broad St., Hazleton.
E. J. McKernan, 9 W. Diamond Ave., Hazleton.
Mrs. E. J. McKernan, 9 W. Diamond Ave., Hazleton.
Mr. E. F. Warner, Weatherly.
Mrs. E. F. Warner, Weatherly.
G. J. Bruger, Freeland.
Mrs. G. J. Bruger, Freeland.
Nell R. McLaughlin, 8 West First St., Hazleton.
L. C. Scott, Lansford.
Mrs. L. C. Scott, Lansford.
Dr. I. E. Freyman, Weatherly.
Mrs. I. E. Freyman, Weatherly.
Mrs. A. D. Hoebner, 70 S. Wyoming St., Hazleton.
Mrs. Percy Faust, Weatherly.
Percy M. Faust, Weatherly.
W. W. Wayne, R. D., Weatherly.

Central District:

D. A. Mackin, Retreat.
W. J. Trembath, 368 N. Maple Ave., Kingston.
Thomas Turner, Sr., 87 Robert St., Alden.
Rosser Mainwaring, 232 Miners Bank Bldg., Wilkes-Barre.
Elizabeth Hopson, Wilkes-Barre.
J. H. Evans, Forty Fort, Kingston.
Miss Mary Moore, Plymouth.
Miss Helen Newman, Wilkes-Barre.
Miss Florence Wilson, Wilkes-Barre.

Pittston Poor District:

I. C. Owen, Taylor.
C. W. Smiles, 178 Fulton St., Pittston.

General:

Lt. Gov. Arthur H. James, Plymouth.
Chas. F. Johnson, Kislyn.
O. C. Whitaker, 59 N. Church St., Hazleton.
Miss Ethel May, 535 N. Vine St., Hazleton.
Miss Gertrude Pardee Kellar, Hazleton.
Miss Neil A. Fountain, Wilkes-Barre.
John H. Bigelow, Hazleton.
Mrs. Wm. M. Dyatt, Church St., Hazleton.
Wm. M. Dyatt, Church St., Hazleton.
Mrs. Mary Clark, Hazleton.
Mayor James G. Harvey, Hazleton.
M. S. James, 117 W. Second St., Hazleton.
John Leffler, Hazleton.
Dr. R. E. Buckley, Hazleton.
Anna Bock, Hazleton.
Pasco Schiavo, Hazleton.
August Mitke, Hazleton.

LUZERNE COUNTY—Cont.

Harry F. Grebey, Hazleton.
Max Friedlander, Hazleton.
Atty. John H. Bonnin, Hazleton.
Eckley B. Markle, Hazleton.
Rev. Robert B. Jack, Hazleton.
Rev. Joseph H. Price, Hazleton.
Charles Wilde, Hazleton.
G. Stewart Engle, Hazleton.
P. F. Loughran, Hazleton.
M. J. Lyman, Hazleton.
D. T. McKelvey, Hazleton.

LYCOMING COUNTY

E. E. Ohl, Williamsport.
Mrs. E. E. Ohl, Williamsport.

MERCER COUNTY

W. W. Dight, Mercer.
J. H. McKean, Sheakleyville.
Mrs. J. H. McKean, Sheakleyville.
J. P. Griffith, 85 S. Water, Sharon.
T. C. White, Mercer.
Mrs. T. C. White, Mercer.
C. K. Shaffer, Stoneboro.
Mrs. M. Stewart, Stoneboro.

MIFFLIN COUNTY

W. A. McNitt, Walnut St., Reedsville.
Mitchell M. Bricker, Chestnut St., Lewistown.
Daniel Brought, Lewistown.

MONTGOMERY COUNTY

W. C. Irvin, Court House, Norristown.
Ralph McLaughlin, 713 W. Oak St., Norristown.
Dr. W. Z. Anders, Collegeville.
Mrs. W. Z. Anders, Collegeville.
Mrs. Euphemia C. Dunn, N. Glenside.
F. K. Moore, Norristown.
H. R. Thomas, Royersford.
Mrs. H. R. Thomas, Royersford.
Martin L. Horn, Royersford.
Mrs. Martin L. Horn, Royersford.
J. Wayne Heebner, R. D. 5, Norristown.

MONROE COUNTY

Edward G. Gerhard, Stroudsburg.
Mrs. Edward G. Gerhard, Stroudsburg.

NORTHAMPTON COUNTY

Steward L. Houck, 2126 Greensburg Ave., Easton.
Clarence Holland, Nazareth.
Eugene Achenbach, Wind Gap.

NORTHUMBERLAND COUNTY

C. A. Ambrose, 1225 Chestnut St., Kulpmont.
Lemuel Griffith, 46 S. Maple St., Mt. Carmel.

PHILADELPHIA COUNTY

Francis X. Hogan, 1526 Willington St., Philadelphia.
Mrs. Lena Roberts, 1733 Vine St., Philadelphia.
Edwin D. Solenberger, 311 S. Juniper St., Philadelphia.
G. R. Bedinger, 311 S. Juniper St., Philadelphia.
Miss A. F. Brownell, 311 S. Juniper St., Philadelphia.
Horace Wolstenholme, 5244 10th St., Philadelphia.
Edward Plankington, Philadelphia.
Wm. J. Wahl, 2723 W. Thompson Ave., Philadelphia.

Roxborough Poor District:

Harry H. Markley, Ridge & Manatona Ave., Roxborough.
Nathan L. Jones, 5845 Ridge Ave., Roxborough.
Dr. Clarence Dengler, 3201 Ridge Ave., Wissahicken.
Josiah Staneruck, Supt. Roxborough Poor House, Roxborough.
Mrs. Elizabeth Staneruck, Matron Roxborough Poor House, Roxborough.
George E. Dorwart, 6222 Ridge Ave., Philadelphia.

Bristol Poor District:

E. S. Ward, 153 West Tabor Road, Philadelphia.
Arthur G. Graham, 60 Seventh Ave., Oak Lane, Philadelphia.
George W. Hankinson, 7130 N. Broad St., Philadelphia.
Chas. P. Sanville, 1456 Sparks St., Philadelphia.
N. J. Dilworth, 4915 N. 13th St., Philadelphia.
Harry G. Rintz, 5401 N. Lawrence St., Olney.
Mrs. F. M. Henson, 2025 Medary Ave., Philadelphia.

Oxford and Lower Dublin:

Mr. and Mrs. Casper M. Titus, 6946 Torresdale Ave., Tacony, Phila.
Mrs. G. H. Croft, 1528 Overington St., Frankford, Philadelphia.
Harry L. Buckius, 1528 Overington St., Frankford, Philadelphia.
Mrs. Harry L. Buckius, 1528 Overington St., Frankford, Philadelphia.
R. M. Corson, Philadelphia.
Wm. J. Hill, 5421 Oakland St., Philadelphia.
Mr. and Mrs. Lewis F. Castor, Jr., 1504 Harrison St., Frankford, Phila.
James L. Adams, 4728 Griscom St., Philadelphia.
Mr. and Mrs. Frank M. Mooney, 7963 Oxford Ave., Fox Chase, Phila.
Mr. and Mrs. Wm. G. Ewald, 942 E. Bustleton Ave., Philadelphia.
Mrs. Naomi Kelly, Cottman St., Holmesburg, Philadelphia.
Samuel L. Kelly, Cottman St., Holmesburg, Philadelphia.
George A. Williams, 1026 Foulkrod St., Frankford, Philadelphia.
Mrs. Carl Ebert, 8024 Jackson St., Holmesburg, Philadelphia.
Mr. and Mrs. John J. McKeough, Linden Ave., State Rd., Torresdale.
Carl Ebert, 8024 Jackson St., Holmesburg, Philadelphia.

Germantown Poor District:

Thomas A. Conolly, 204 E. Evergreen Ave., Germantown, Philadelphia.
James T. McClellan, 131 E. Chelten Ave., Germantown, Philadelphia.
J. Wesley Craig, 374 Shedaker St., Germantown.
John Marsden, 11 Mermaid Lane. Germantown.
Paul Reilly, Esq., 1516 Chestnut St., Germantown.
Mrs. Emily L. Carmichael, 20 E. Gowen Ave., Mt. Airy, Philadelphia.
Frank Linck, Rittenhouse St. & Pulaskie Ave., Germantown.
James L. Tyler, 104 Pastorius St., Germantown.
Harry Berger, 5314 Wayne Ave., Germantown.

TIOGA COUNTY

Mr. and Mrs. Joseph Hughes, Wellsboro.
Mr. and Mrs. Ralph Baity, Wellsboro.
Mr. and Mrs. F. E. Reinwald, Wellsboro.

UNION COUNTY

D. R. Crossgrove, Lewisburg.
Blaine O. Catherman, Hartleton.
F. B. Reigel, Winfield.
Thomas A. Spangler, R. D. 1, Lewisburg.
G. T. Biehl, Lewisburg.
Mrs. Ruth M. Steece, Mifflinburg.

VENANGO COUNTY

Lura Crain, R. F. D. 5, Venango.
Fred Gates, 401 W. First St., Oil City.
Charles W. King, Cooperstown.
T. B. Baker, Franklin.
Mrs. Fred Tate, 1208 Myrtle St., Franklin.
Fred Tate, 1208 Myrtle St., Franklin.

WARREN COUNTY

Mrs. E. M. Lowe, Sugar Grove.
E. M. Lowe, Sugar Grove, Warren.
M. Brady and Mrs. M. Brady, Youngville.
H. P. Ridelspèrger, Warren.
E. D. Stewart, Warren.
Mrs. E. D. Stewart, Warren.
Mr. and Mrs. G. E. Seavy, Warren.
Mrs. H. P. Ridelsperger, Warren.

WASHINGTON COUNTY

D. Glenn Moore, 43 North Ave., Washington.
Mr. and Mrs. T. C. Luellen, R. D. 9, Washington.
Harry A. Jones, Esq., 522 Wash. Trust Bldg., Washington.
Mr. and Mrs. R. C. Buchanan, 184 Duncan Ave., Washington.
Elizabeth Christman, Washington.
Mrs. Lillian M. Lane, Washington.
Chas. R. Riggle, R. D. 9, Washington.
Mrs. C. R. Riggle, R. D. 9, Washington.
Elizabeth H. Wilson, 103 LeMoyne Ave., Washington.

WESTMORELAND COUNTY

Mr. and Mrs. J. S. Hamberg, Irwin.
Mr. and Mrs. J. B. Robinson, Greensburg.
Mr. and Mrs. Ed. Klingensmith, Vandergrift.

OTHER STATES

Dr. C. C. Carstens, New York City.
Carl M. Johns, Elmira, New York.
J. C. Cuttwell, 3130 South Canal St, Chicago.
Mrs. Cornelia B. Meytrott, State Office Bldg., Trenton, N. J.

CHARTER

Copy of Charter Granted October 19, 1914, to the Association of Directors of the Poor and Charities and Corrections of the State of Pennsylvania.

CORPORATION OF THE FIRST CLASS

Petition for Corporation

To The Honorable William H. Ruppel, President Judge of the Court of Common Pleas of Somerset County, Pennsylvania:

In compliance with the requirements of The Act of the General Assembly of the Commonwealth of Pennsylvania, "An Act to provide for the Corporation and Regulation of certain Corporations," approved the 29th day of April, Anno Domini, one Thousand Eight Hundred and seventy-four and its supplements, the undersigned, Andrew S. Miller, Esq., Francis J. Torrance, S. A. Cramer, James McB. Robb, R. C. Buchanan, John L. Smith, Oliver P. Bohler, H. D. Browneller, James L. Reilly, Fred Fuller, J. W. Peck, Dr. W. A. Paine, P. H. Holler, Mrs. Sue Willard, Mrs. Mildred S. Lindsey, Mrs. Abbie W. Wilder, E. Thompson, Dr. B. A. Black, Addison White, Philip Hartzog, J. H. Flaherty, Chas. F. Loesel, Frank J. Dickert, W. C. Grube, A. S. Brubaker, F. M. Ainsley, D. A. Mackin, P. G. Cober, Esq., J. W. Smith, M. Brady, I. C. Colburn, Esq., E. D. Solenberger, Miss Florence D. Cameron, Dr. R. W. Wolfe, J. M. Stauffer, E. E. Ohl, W. G. Theurer, Miss Belle Chalfant, Mrs. Mary Hughes Ewing, Dr. M. P. Barr, Dr. J. M. Murdock, Mrs. J. L. Anderson and others who are citizens of Pennsylvania, having associated themselves together for the purpose hereinafter specified and desiring that they may be duly incorporated, according to law, do hereby certify:

FIRST:—The name of the corporation shall be, "Association of Directors of the Poor and Charities and Correction of the State of Pennsylvania."

SECOND:—The said corporation is formed for the purpose of discussing all questions pertaining to the care and management of County Homes, Hospitals, and Institutions, the suppression of pauperism and crime, idiocy, feeble-mindedness and insanity, the spread of disease and crime, the care, of neglected, delinquent, deformed and afflicted children, the care, training, maintenance and nursing of the idiotic, feeble-minded and insane of the State, to suggest and advocate such legislation as will be helpful in carrying out the object and purposes, reform the wayward, correct the delinquents and care for the affliced and advocate and adopt such measures as may tend to the building up of a better citizenship, morally, physically and intellectually, to meet annually in convention at some designated point within the Commonwealth where these objects and purposes and the questions pertaining to them may be discussed for the better preparing those who are entrusted with the care of the classes herein recited, and recommending to the board of public charities and the Legislature, such legislation as should be passed, and for better preparing those for the discharge of their duties, the making and adopting of by-laws for the government and regulation of the corporation and its members, and for these purposes to have, possess and enjoy all the rights, benefits and privilegesof the said Act of Assembly aforesaid and its supplement.

THIRD:—The place or places where the convention of The Association is to be held and the business of the said corporation is to be transacted is at such place, city or borough, in the State as may be designated by the members of the association in convention for the previous year.

FOURTH:—The corporation shall have perpetual existence.

FIFTH:—The names and residences of the subscribers hereto are as follows.

Name	Post Office	County
Andrew S. Miller	Pittsburgh	Allegheny
Francis J. Torrance	Pittsburgh	Allegheny
W. G. Theurer	Washington	Washington
R. W. Wolfe	Taylorstown	Washington
H. D. Browneller	W. Brownsville	Washington
John McNary	Washington	Washington
Jas. W. Smith	Peckville	Lackawanna
F. B. Bausman	Lancaster	Lancaster
Willard Mathews	Scranton	Lackawanna
Philip Hartzog	Carrolltown	Cambria
W. A. Paine	Scranton	Lackawanna
R. C. Buchanan	Washington	Washington
Robert Barclay	Johnstown	Cambria
P. H. Holler	Chambersburg	Franklin
A. S. Brubaker	Lancaster	Lancaster
I. H. Mayer	Waynesboro	Franklin
J. W. Peck	Meyersdale	Somerset
Chas. F. Loesel	Erie	Erie
P. G. Cober	Somerset	Somerset
M. P. Whitaker	Narvon	Lancaster
D. A. Mackin	Retreat	Luzerne
E. E. Ohl	Williamsport	Lycoming
James McB. Robb	Oakdale	Allegheny
E. D. Solenberger	Philadelphia	Philadelphia
Hettie Porch	Arden	Washington
J. H. Flaherty	Pittsburgh	Allegheny
Wm. J. McGarry	Philadelphia	Philadelphia
James M. Norris	Warrendale	Allegheny
S. A. Cramer	Warren	Warren
E. E. Thompson	Warren	Warren
M. Brady	Youngsville	Warren
Addison White	Warren	Warren

Name	Post Office	County
Mildred S. Lindsey	Warren	Warren
Fred Fuller	Scranton	Lackawanna
B. A. Black	Polk	Venango
Anna L. Bohan Barret	Pittston	Luzerne
Thomas F. Mumford	Centralia	Columbia
John Barrett	Glen Lyon	Luzerne
John B. Clark	Luzerne	Luzerne
James L. Reilly	Ashley	Luzerne
Juliette Campbell	Butler	Butler
Belle C. Chalfant	Pittsburgh	Allegheny
F. J. Dickert	Scranton	Lackawanna
John J. Kenney	Parsons	Luzerne
Mrs. Sue Willard	Indiana	Indiana
E. M. Ainsley	Indiana	Indiana
Oliver P. Bohler	Philadelphia	Philadelphia
Albert P. Roderus	Rankin	Allegheny
Florence D. Cameron	Lincoln University	Chester
John L. Smith	Chester Springs	Chester
L. C. Colborn	Somerset	Somerset
Geo. F. Kimmel	Somerset	Somerset

The membership of the corporation shall be composed of the Directors, Guardians and Overseers of the Poor or County Commissioners acting as such, of the Poor Directors of Pennsylvania, physicians, solicitors, clerks and matrons and all officers of almshouses, the Governor and heads of Departments of the State, the judges of the several courts of Pennsylvania, members of the State Board of Public Charities.   Committee on Lunacy. Trustees, physicians. superintendent and managers of all insane hospitals, training schools for feeble-minded, trustees and officers of children's homes, schools for the blind, institutions for the deaf and dumb, reformatory and industrial schools, Children's Aid Societies, societies for the prevention of cruelty, probation officers, and all persons connected with charitable, benevolent and corrective institutions and associations, all trustees, officers, physicians and nurses, of all hospitals for the care of the sick, maimed and injured and transmittable diseases.

SIXTH:—The business of the corporation is to be managed by the officers of the association, consisting of a President, Seven Vice-Presidents, Secretary, Assistant Secretary, Honorary Secretary and Treasurer.

The President, First Vice-President, the Secretary, Assistant Secretary and Treasurer, shall compose the Executive Committee.

The names and residences of those chosen as officers to serve for one year are as follows:

D. A. Mackin, President, Retreat, Luzerne Co.; Vice-Presidents—Bromley Wharton, Philadelphia, Philadelphia Co.; Frank P. Bausman, Laneaster, Lancaster Co.; John H. Flaherty, Pittsburgh, Allegheny Co.; M. Brady, Youngsville, Warren Co.; Mrs. Reed Teitrich, Carlisle, Cumberland Co.; Miss Belle Chalfant, Pittsburgh, Allegheny Co.; Miss Florence Cameron, Lincoln University, Chester Co.; Chas. Snyder, Philadelphia, Philadelphia Co.; J. M. Stauffer, Hazleton, Luzerne Co.; R. D. Wolfe, Taylortown, Washington Co.; T. C. White, Mercer, Mercer Co.; Oliver P. Bohler, Philadelphia, Philadelphia Co.; L. C. Colborn, Esq., Secretary and Treasurer, Somerset, Somerset Co.; Edwin D. Solenberger, Asst. Sec., Philadelphia, Philadelphia Co.; Fred Fuller, Hon. Sec., Scranton, Lackawanna Co.

SEVENTH:—The names and residences of the officers chosen who will compose the executive committee to serve for one year are as follows:

D. A. Mackin, President, Retreat, Pa.; Bromley Wharton, Vice-President, Philadelphia; Miss Belle Chalfant, Vice-President, Pittsburgh, Pa.; L. C. Colborn, Sec'y and Treas., Somerset; Edwin D. Solenberger, Assistant Secretary, Philadelphia; Fred Fuller, Honorary Secretary, Scranton.

EIGHTH:—The corporation has no capital stock to be held in shares.

NINTH:—The yearly income of the corporation will not exceed Three Thousand Dollars. The work of the association is purely charitable, benevolent and philanthropic in character, its funds to be used for the purpose of paying the expenses of holding the annual conventions, stenographic services for reporting the proceedings, printing the reports of the proceedings of the convention, printing of programs, postage, stationery, expenses of Secretary and Treasurer and the paying of such other expenses that may be connected with the business of the association, and for securing experienced speakers to deliver addresses at the convention on such questions as may be designated by the Executive Committee, the funds necessary to defray these expenses to be raised by voluntary assessments, levied upon the various almshouses, hospitals and poor districts, institutions through the State, or by appropriation made by the State, or by donation or gift to the Association.

WITNESS our hands and seals this 8th day of October, A. D. 1914.

Andrew S. Miller,	(SEAL)	E. E. Ohl,	(SEAL)
J. H. Flaherty,	(SEAL)	Geo. F. Kimmel,	(SEAL)
W. G. Theurer,	(SEAL)	James M. Norris,	(SEAL)
Wm. J. McGarry,	(SEAL)	S. A. Cramer,	(SEAL)
Hettie Porch,	(SEAL)	E. E. Thompson,	(SEAL)
R. W. Wolfe,	(SEAL)	Addison White,	(SEAL)
M. Brady,	(SEAL)	E. M. Ainsley,	(SEAL)
Mildred S. Lindsey,	(SEAL)	John McNary,	(SEAL)

Fred Fuller,	(SEAL)	D. A. Mackin,	(SEAL)
Francis J. Torrance,	(SEAL)	J. McB. Robb,	(SEAL)
B. A. Black,	(SEAL)	Albert P. Roderus,	(SEAL)
E. D. Solenberger,	(SEAL)	P. H. Holler,	(SEAL)
Anna L. Bohan Barrett,	(SEAL)	John L. Smith,	(SEAL)
John B. Clark,	(SEAL)	Mary Hughes Ewing,	(SEAL)
T. C. White,	(SEAL)	J. W. Peck,	(SEAL)
Juliette Campbell,	(SEAL)	J. M. Stauffer,	(SEAL)
Belle Chalfant,	(SEAL)	W. C. Grube,	(SEAL)
F. J. Dickert,	(SEAL)	Robert Barclay,	(SEAL)
Willard Mathews,	(SEAL)	F B Bausman,	(SEAL)
John J. Kenney,	(SEAL)	A. S. Brubaker,	(SEAL)
Mrs. Sue Willard,	(SEAL)	L. C. Colborn,	(SEAL)
Jas. W. Smith,	(SEAL)	P. G. Cober,	(SEAL)
R. C. Buchanan,	(SEAL)	Philip Hartzog,	(SEAL)
H. D. Browneller,	(SEAL)	Charles F. Loesel,	(SEAL)
Oliver P. Bohler,	(SEAL)	J. H. Moyer,	(SEAL)
Florence D. Cameron,	(SEAL)	N. A. Paine,	(SEAL)
Abbie W. Wilder,	(SEAL)	M. P. Whitaker,	(SEAL)

COMMONWEALTH OF PENNSYLVANIA,
  COUNTY OF SOMERSET, ss

Before me the subscriber, Recorder of Deeds in and for the County of Somerset, personally appeared P. G. Cober, Geo. F. Kimmel and L. C. Colburn, three of the subscribers to the above foregoing certificate of Incorporation, The Association of Directors of the Poor and Charities and Corrections of the State of Pennsylvania, and in due form of law acknowledged the same to be their act and deed and desired that same might be recorded as such.

WITNESS my hand and official seal this 19th day of October, A. D. 1914.

JOHN G. EMERT (SEAL)
SOMERSET COUNTY, ss: Recorder of Deeds.

L. C. Colborn, Geo. F. Kimmel and P. G. Cober, being duly sworn as the law directs, say that the above advertisement has been published for three successive weeks in the Somerset Herald and the Somerset Standard, two newspapers of general circulation, printed in the County of Somerset as follows: In the Somerset Herald on the days of 21st and 28th of October and 4th of November, 1914, and in the Somerset Standard on the 22nd and 29th of October and the 5th of November, 1914, and further that the subscribers to the said charter here presented are all citizens of the Commonwealth of Pennsylvania, sworn and subscribed before me this 19th day of October, 1914.

P. G. COBER,
GEO. F. KIMMEL,
L. C. COLBORN.

In the Court of Common Pleas of Somerset County, Pennsylvania, of No.   December Term 1914.

And now this 10th day of November, 1914, the within charter and certificate of incorporation having been presented to me, a Law Judge of Somerset County, accompanied by due proof of publication of the notice of this application as required by the Act of Assembly and rule of this Court in such case made and provided, I certify that I have examined and perused the said writing, and have found the same to be in proper form, and within the purpose named in the first-class specified in section second of the Act of the General Assembly of the Commonwealth of Pennsylvania, entitled "An Act to provide for the Incorporation and regulation of certain Corporations," approved April 29th, 1874, and the supplements thereto, and the same appearing to be lawful and not injurious to the community, I do hereby on motion of L. C. Colborn, Esquire, on behalf of the petitioners, order and direct that the said charter of "Association of Directors of the Poor and Charities and Corrections of the State of Pennsylvania" aforesaid be and the same is hereby approved and that upon the recording of the same and of this order the subscribers thereto, and their associates shall be a corporation by name of "Association of Directors of the Poor and Charities and Corrections of the State of Pennsylvania," for the purposes and upon the terms herein stated.

W. H. RUPPELL, President Judge.

Recorded in the office for recording of deeds in and for the County of Somerset, in Deed Book Volume 192, Page 180.

WITNESS my hand and seal of office this 14th day of Nov., 1914.

JOHN G. EMERT,   (SEAL)
Recorder of Deeds.

BY-LAWS*

Of the Association of Directors of the Poor and Charities and Corrections of the State of Pennsylvania.

Name

Section 1.   The Association shall be known as "The Association of Directors of the Poor and Charities and Corrections of Pennsylvania."

---

*Adopted at Johnstown, Pa., October 17, 1917, and amended as to Section 7 at Williamsport, Pa., October 17, 1923.

Membership

Sec. 2. The membership of the Association shall consist of Directors, Guardians and Overseers of the Poor of the several poor districts of the State, attorneys and clerks of such Boards of Directors, Guardians and Overseers, physicians, superintendents, stewards and officers of the Alms-houses, the Judges of the Courts, the members, officers and agents of the Board of Public Charities, the Trustees, superintendents and managers and other officers of Hospitals for the Insane, training schools for the feeble-minded, trustees and officers of children's homes and correctional or training schools and institutions for the blind, deaf and dumb, all officers and members of Children's Aid Societies, probation officers and all persons connected with any charitable, benevolent or correctional institutions or societies.

Sec. 3. The Officers of the Association shall consist of a President, seven Vice-Presidents, Secretary, two Assistant Secretaries, and two Honorary Secretaries and a Treasurer, who shall be elected annually and hold their respective offices for a period of one year or until their successors have been elected and signified their acceptance of such office.

The President

Sec. 4. The President shall preside at the meetings of the Convention and all called or special meetings of the Association, except when same is delegated to the chairman of a sectional meeting. He shall be governed in the discharge of his duties by such parliamentary rules as are recognized as authority. At the first business meeting of each annual Convention, he shall appoint Committees as follows:

1. Committee of seven members which shall be designated as "Committee on Officers."

2. Committee of three members which shall be designated as "Auditing Committee."

3. Committee of seven members designated as "Committee on Place of Holding Next Convention."

4. Committee of ten members designated as the "Committee on Resolutions."

The incoming President each year shall appoint within thirty days after the Annual Meeting of the Association a Committee of five members designated as a "Committee on Legislation."

The Executive Committee

Sec. 5. The Executive Committee shall consist of the President and First Vice-President, the other Officers of the Association and the Chairman of the Committee on Legislation and the last three ex-presidents as ex-officio members.

The Executive Committee shall be responsible for the Program of the Annual Convention and shall have power to appoint such Sub-Committee as they may deem necessary to assist in providing the program. Three members shall constitute a quorum of this Committee.

Time of Holding Convention

Sec. 6. The Association shall hold its Annual Convention in October of each year at such as may be fixed by the Executive Committee.

Receipts and Expenditures

Sec. 7. The funds necessary to defray the expenses of holding the Convention and attending to the business of the Association shall be raised as follows, to be divided into four classes.

1. By an assessment of $30.00 to be levied upon each County Poor District, State or Semi-State Institution or Society.

2. By an assessment of $20.00 to be levied upon larger Township or Municipal Poor Districts and Private Institution or Societies.

3. By an assessment of $10.00 to be levied upon the smaller Township and Borough Poor Districts or smaller Institutions or Societies..

4. By annual dues of $5.00 to be paid by those who wish to register as individual members.

The Executive Committee shall have power to reduce the amount of any particular class named in this Section and to decide to which of the several classes each Poor District, Institution or Organization belongs.

Duties of Officers and Committees

Sec. 8. 1—The President shall preside at the meetings of the Convention, appoint all Committees except as otherwise provided, and have general supervision of the work of the Association.

The Vice-Presidents, in the order named, shall preside in the absence of the President.

2. The Secretary shall have charge of the records of the Association, except those of the Treasurer, give notice of meetings to the members, notify all persons on the program of the part assigned to them, see that the minutes and the reports are printed and distributed, and perform all other duties and services as shall be required by the Executive Committee and for such services the Association is to pay him such amount as may be fixed by the Association at each Convention, and in addition he shall receive payment for all necessary expenses incident thereto.

3. The Assistant Secretaries shall assist the Secretary in the performance of his duties when required, and when called to go on any business for the Convention their expenses shall be paid by the Association.

4. The Honorary Secretaries shall be advisory in their duties, and shall assist in promoting the best interest of the Association.

5. The Treasurer shall send out all assessments to the various Directors of the Poor, Institutions, Schools and Societies, and collect and give a proper receipt for same, keep an account of all monies so collected and pay out the same on written approval by the President and Secretary and each year he shall present his report in full to the Auditing Committee to be audited by them, and for his services the Association is to pay him such amount as may be fixed by the Association at each Convention, and in addition he shall receive payment for all necessary expenses incident thereto.

6. The Treasurer shall give a surety bond in the sum of $1000.00 (One Thousand Dollars) the expense of same to be borne by the Association.

7. The Executive Committee shall arrange the business of the Association and shall have general supervision of the Association and its best interests.

General Provisions

Sec. 9. 1.—The Executive Committee shall arrange with the Local Committee in each city where the Convention meets for a suitable badge for the Association for each Annual Convention.

2. The Committee on Legislation shall keep in touch with any pending legislation pertaining to the classes represented by the Association and shall report at the Annual Convention in regard to the same.

Amendments

Sec. 10. These By-Laws may be amended by the members at any annual meeting at the Convention, by a two-third vote of all the members present, providing that notice of such amendment be given in writing to each member of the Executive Committee at least ten days before the Annual Meeting and the same to be presented to the Convention at least one full day before final action by the Convention.

Order of Business—Opening Meeting

Sec. 11. 1.—Meeting at time and place, and calling to order by the President.
2. Music.
3. Devotional Exercises.
4. Address of Welcome.
5. Response to Address of Welcome.
6. President's Address.
7. Announcements.
8. Adjournment.

Regular Meeting

2. Music if provided.
3. Miscellaneous Business.
4. New Business.
5. Regular Program.
6. Reports of Committee.

HISTORICAL STATEMENT

In the fall of 1875, through the efforts of Messrs. R. D. McGonnigle, and D. C. Hultz, of the Allegheny City Home, a number of persons interested in almshouses and hospitals for the insane met informally and agreed upon the organization of an "Association of Directors of the Poor and Public Charities." Among others at this meeting were John Herron, J. W. Bell, Henry Chalfant, Dr. J. B. Johnson, L. S. Wainwright and Luther Bakewell, then Secretary of the State Board of Public Charities. The almshouses and hospitals for the insane throughout the State were discussed and their condition was described as being "deplorable." It was agreed that a call be made for a convention to be held in Altoona on the 19th of January, 1876. At this first meeting of the convention, ten counties of the State were represented. On September 19, 1876—the same year—the second meeting was held in Lancaster. Since then, beginning with 1877, annual meetings or conventions have been held in the month of October down to the present time, except in 1918 when the influenza epidemic and war conditions made it necessary to postpone the Butler Convention until 1919·

On October 1914 a Charter was granted by the Somerset County Courts to the Association of Directors of the Poor and Charities and Corrections of Pennsylvania. Act No. 266 of July 6, 1917, (P. L. 734), approved by Gov. Martin G. Brumbaugh, authorized the Directors, officers and staff of the various Poor Districts to attend the annual meetings as a part of their official duties and provided for the payment of their necessary expenses in so doing. The Act also provided for the payment of a membership subscription for the support of the Convention not to exceed $15.00 per annum. Act No. 36, approved by Governor Gifford Pinchot, April 4, 1923, (P. L. 58), amended the above Act as to Section 2 by striking out $15.00 and inserting in place thereof $30.00—thus authorizing the Poor Districts to pay a membership subscription for any Poor District not to exceed $30.00 per annum for the purposes named in Section 2 of the Act of July 6, 1917. A complete list of the various places of meeting follows:

Preliminary meeting for organization—Fall of 1875 in Allegheny City.

No.	Place	Date
1	Altoona	Jannary 19, 1876
2	Lancaster	September 19, 1876
3	Lock Haven	1877
4	Pittsburgh	1878
5	Scranton	1879
6	Harrisburg	1880
7	Erie	1881
8	Somerset	1882
9	Philadelphia	1883
10	Greensburg	1884
11	Philadelphia	1885

No.	Place	Date
12	Scranton	1886
13	Gettysburg	1887
14	Uniontown	1888
15	Altoona	1889
16	Lancaster	1890
17	Reading	1891
18	Erie	1892
19	Williamsport	1893
20	York	1894
21	Philadelphia	1895
22	Pittsburgh	1896
23	Scranton	1897
24	Harrisburg	1898
25	Erie	1899
26	Wilkes-Barre	1900
27	Altoona	1901
28	Somerset	1902
29	Lancaster	1903
30	Gettysburg	1904
31	Washington	1905
32	Warren	1906
33	Meadville	1907
34	West Chester	1908
35	Bradford	1909
36	Williamsport	1910
37	Indiana	1911
38	Erie	1912
39	Philadelphia	1913
40	Carlisle	1914
41	Reading	1915
42	Altoona	1916
43	Johnstown	1917
	Meeting omitted on account of influenza epidemic	1918
44	Butler	1919
45	Harrisburg	1920
46	Wilkes-Barre	1921
47	Uniontown	1922
48	Williamsport	1923
49	Washington	1924
50	Lancaster	1925
51	Erie	1926
52	Hazleton	1927

AN ACT—NO. 266—P.L. 734 of JULY 6, 1917, as
Amended By Act No. 36—P.L. 58 of April 4, 1923.

Authorizing the directors and overseers of the poor or other officers having
charge of the poor in the poor districts of this Commonwealth together
with their solicitor steward or superintendent and such other executive
officer as may designate by said directors and overseers or other officers
to attend the annual meeting of the association of directors of the poor
and charities and corrections of Pennsylvania as part of their official
duties and providing for the payment of the expenses thereof

Section   1   *Be it enacted by the Senate and House of Representatives of
the Commonwealth of Pennsylvania in General Assembly met and it is hereby
enacted by the authority of the same* · That the directors and overseers of
the poor or other officers having charge of the poor in the poor districts
of this Commonwealth together with their solicitor steward or superintend-,
ent and such other executive officers as may be designated by said directors
and overseers or other officers are hereby authorized as part of their official
duties to attend the annual meeting of the association of directors of the
poor and charities and corrections of Pennsylvania for the purpose of discussing the various questions arising in the discharge of their duties and
of providing for uniform and economical methods of administering the
affairs of the respective poor districts

Section   2   The actual expenses of the aforesaid officials attending the
said annual meetings of said association including traveling expenses and
hotel bills actually paid by them together with a membership subscription
by each poor district to the necessary expenses of the convention including
printing employment, of stenographers and expenses of committees which
said membership subscription however shall not be more than thirty dollars
for any poor district per annum shall be paid out of the funds of the poor
district   The time spent in attending such meeting shall not be more than
four days exclusive of the time employed in traveling thereto and therefrom

APPENDIX
ON
DIET IN THE COUNTY HOME.
(See pages 69-73)

CANNING AND STORAGE BUDGET.

I. Vegetables

    A.   **Every person needs 2 Vegetables a Day other than Potatoes:** such as carrots, string beans, beets, peas, corn, asparagus, onions, lima beans.

    B.   **Greens**—twice a week such as spinach, kale, Swiss chard, beet tops, New Zealand spinach, wild greens.

    C.   **Tomatoes**—twice a week.

    D.   **A raw vegetable twice a week** such as cabbage, lettuce, raw carrots, celery, endive, dandelion, Chinese cabbage, cut leaf chicory.

    E.   Use occasionally corn, dried beans, squash, and parsnips.

II. Fruits

    A.   Every person needs also two canned, dried, or fresh fruits a day.

A DAY'S FOOD PLAN FOR AN ELDERLY PERSON

Age: 70—80   Fuel Requirement: 1500—1800 Calories

Time	Food	Calories
7:30 A.M.	Soft, sweet fruit or mild, diluted fruit juice, (grape, pineapple, or apple)	75—100 Calories
	Well-cooked cereal with thin cream and a little sugar............	100—200 Calories
	Toast or zwieback with butter....	100—200 Calories
	Bacon or soft-cooked eggs........	75—150 Calories
	Tea or coffee with cream and sugar	100—200 Calories
12:30 P.M.	Cream soup..................	100—150 Calories
	Fish or oysters, cheese souffle or fondue........................	100—200 Calories
	A cooked green vegetable finely chopped......................	10—25 Calories
	Rice, or baked or riced potato.....	75—100 Calories
	Toast or zwieback with butter....	100—200 Calories
	Stewed fruit or fruit jelly with gelatin or tapioca................	100—200 Calories
4:P.M.	Tea or coffee, or bouillon, or malted milk, toast or crackers......	75—100 Calories
6 P.M.	Chicken, or lamb chop, or broiled beef balls......................	100—150 Calories
	Riced, or baked, or mashed potato	75—100 Calories
	One other cooked vegetable (Soft enough to mash with a fork).......	25—100 Calories
	Toast or swieback, or dinner biscuit............................	75—100 Calories
	Custard, or cereal pudding, or gelatin dessert....................	100—200 Calories
	Tea or coffee with cream and sugar	100—200 Calories

6 A.M.	Weak tea or coffee with hot milk or cream or hot milk or malted milk....	75—100 Calories
8 A.M.	Soft-cooked egg or omelet or well-cooked cereal with cream..........	75—150 Calories
	Zwieback or toast..............	75—150 Calories
	Weak tea or coffee with hot milk or cream.......................	75—100 Calories
12:30 P.M.	Cream soup or vegetable puree with croutons...................	100—200 Calories
	Broiled, baked, ·or boiled fish,) small servings or) Cheese souffle or egg timbale)	100—200 Calories
	Baked, riced, or mashed potato...	50—100 Calories
	Stewed or baked fruit............	100—150 Calories
	Weak tea or coffee with hot milk or cream.......................	75—100 Calories
4 P.M.	Tea or coffee with hot milk or cream.........................	75—100 Calories
6 P.M.	Broth.........................	10—15 Calories
	Minced chicken, lamb, mutton, or beef, small serving...............	100—150 Calories
	Zwieback or toast lightly buttered and moistened with hot, salted water	75—150 Calories
	A cooked vegetable, mashed or sifted (as peas, squash, asparagus tips)............................	25—100 Calories
	Cereal pudding or custard.......	100—200 Calories

PLANNING THE FAMILY'S MEAL
EAT WISELY AND BE WELL

A. For each day use—

        1 quart milk for each child
        1 pint milk for each adult
        8 glasses water for each person

B. And from each group below for the day's meals use—

FOOD GROUPS

Regulating Food	Building Food	Energy Giving Foods
Used by body for regulating purposes.	Used by body to build muscle, bone, nerve, blood tissue.	Used by body for energy, warmth, amount depends upon age, weight, occupation, and digestive power.
2 SERVINGS OF FRUITS A DAY	**1 SERVING OF ANY TWO BELOW**	Cereals—½ in form of whole cereals.
Oranges. Grapefruit. Lemon juice. Bananas. Apples. Pears. Prunes. Dates.	Protein. Milk, cheese, eggs, meats, fish. Cereals, peas, beans, nuts. (cereals must have milk added.) Lime. Milk, cheese, eggs, spinach, celery, lettuce, cabbage, onions, swiss chard. Iron. green vegetables, fruits, cereal—whole grain—eggs. Phosphorous. Milk, eggs, meat, cereal—whole grain—dried peas and beans.	Oatmeal—building. Cracked wheat. Cornmeal. Whole wheat bread. Rye bread. Fats—butter, cream, bacon, eggs, nuts, fat meats. Vegetable Fats—(not as valuable as others, olive oil, etc.) Sweets—(Not to be eaten between meals) Sugar, honey, syrups, jellies and preserves, desserts, candy, etc.
2 SERVINGS OF VEGETABLES A DAY OTHER THAN POTATOES		
Cabbage) One served Lettuce) raw every Celery) day when Onion) possible.		**Starchy Vegetables.** Potatoes, rice, beans, corn, etc.
Spinach or other Greens		**Starchy Fruit.**
Tomatoes, string beans, carrots, onions, cauliflower, turnips, peas, beets.		Bananas.

C. Use variety of foods, so as to be sure of filling body needs.
D. Good cooking helps digestibility of foods.
E. Regular hours for meals make for health.

SUGGESTIONS FOR ·MENUS

BREAKFAST

Orange. Oatmeal and milk. Whole wheat toast and butter. Milk or cocoa.	Baked apple. Shredded wheat. Soft boiled egg. Graham toast and butter. Milk or cocoa.	Rhubarb or other seasonable fruit. Oatmeal and milk. Buttered toast, Milk or cocoa.	Orange. Oatmeal and milk. Graham muffin and butter. Milk or cocoa.

DINNER

Pot roast of beef. Baked potatoes. Creamed carrots. Whole wheat bread. Snow pudding. Milk.	Loin of mutton roast. Browned potatoes. Bread and butter. Escalloped tomatoes. Washington cream pie. Milk.	Meatballs. Scalloped potatoes. Spinach. Bread and butter. Baked apples. and cream. Cookies. Milk.	Irish stew. Cold slaw. Bread and butter. Milk. Canned peaches. Sponge cake. Milk.

SUPPER

Corn chowder. Cabbage and celery salad. Rye bread and butter. Peach butter.	Cream of potato soup. Whole wheat muffins. Dressed lettuce. Nuts and raisins.	Baked rice and tomatoes. Lettuce salad. Graham bread and butter. Cocoa and cookies.	Creamed eggs on toast. Raw carrot, raisin and apple salad. Bran muffins. Milk.

BREAKFAST—Con't.

Prunes. Puffed whole wheat. Buttered toast. Milk or cocoa.	Orange. Pettijohns and milk. Toast and butter. Milk or cocoa.	Grapefruit. Cracked wheat and milk. Bacon. Buttered toast. Milk or cocoa.

DINNER—Con't.

Baked fish.	Liver and bacon.	Chicken.
Egg sauce.	Baked potatoes.	Mashed potatoes.
Boiled potatoes with parsley.	Buttered beets.	Onions.
Bread and butter	Graham bread and butter.	Currant jelly.
String beans.	Cottage pudding.	Oatmeal bread and butter.
Apple pie.	Milk.	Celery and apple salad.
		Ice cream.

SUPPER—Con't.

Macaroni and cheese.	Cream of tomato.	Cheese fondue.
Celery salad.	Egg salad.	Biscuits and butter.
Whole wheat bread and butter.	Toast.	Fruit salad.
Milk.	Hermits.	Cocoa.
Blushing apples.		

Germantown Poor District

hn Marsden, 11 Mermaid Lane, Germantown.
mes F. McClellan, 131 E. Cheiten Ave., Germantown.
rs. Emily L. Carmichael, 20 E. Gowan Ave., Mt. Airy.
ank Linck, Rittenhouse St. & Pulaski Ave., Germantown.

N. J. Dillwort
Arthur G. Gra

Oxf

Roxborough Poor District

orge E. Dorwart, 6222 Ridge Avenue.
siah Staneruck, Roxborough Almshouse, E. Shawmont
    Avenue, Roxborough.

Lewis F. Cast
William G. E
Samuel L. Ke
A. S. Kriebel,

Mrs. Henry Hall Sinnamon, Assistant Director, Department of Public Welf
Mrs. Lena M. Roberts, Chief, Bureau of Personal Assistance, 1733 Vine
Miss Evelyn Cavin, Executive Secretary, Mothers' Assistance Fund for Phil
George W. Elliott, General Secretary, Chamber of Commerce, 12th & Wal
Frank L. Devine, Director of Convention Bureau, Chamber of Commerce,
Miss Ella F. Harris, Council of Social Agencies, Welfare Federation, 311
J. Prentice Murphy, Executive Secretary, Children's Bureau, 311 South J
Dr. I. M. Rubinow, Executive Secretary, Jewish Family Society, 9th & Pin
Mrs. W. Irwin Cheyney, Director Delaware County Poor Board, Media.
Mrs. E. C. Dunn, Director Montgomery County Poor Board, North Glensic
Karl de Schweinitz, General Secretary, Family Society of Philadelphia,
George R. Bedinger, Secretary, Public Charities Association, 311 South Ju
Edward Plankinton, Philadelphia General Hospital, 34th & Spruce Streets.
Edwin D. Solenberger, General Secretary, Children's Aid Society of Pen

PHILADELPHIA HOTEL ACCOMMO

NAME AND ADDRESS	Sin	
HEADQUARTERS	With Bath	Withou
njamin Franklin, Chestnut & Ninth	$4 to $7	......
elphia, 13th & Chestnut Streets	$4 to $6	......
llevue-Stratford, Broad & Walnut	$5 to $8	$4 tc
een's, Eighth & Chestnut	$3.50 to $5	$2 to
tz-Carlton, Broad & Walnut	$6 to $8	......
bert Morris, Seventeenth & Arch	$3 to $4	......
. James, Thirteenth & Walnut	$3.50 to $4	$3
ruce Hotel, Thirteenth & Spruce	$3 to $4	$2.50
lvania Hotel, Juniper & Locust	$4 upward	......
ndig Hotel, Thirteenth & Filbert	$3 to $4	......
alton Hotel, Broad & Locust	$3.50 to $5	$2.50
enton Hotel, Broad & Spruce	$5	$3.50 u

E BENJAMIN FRANKLIN HOTEL, NINTH & CHESTNUT STREETS, is Hea
in the large auditorium, which is well suited for the purpose. This hotel w
ample facilities.

ESERVATIONS SHOULD BE MADE ON OR BEFORE SEPTEMBER 1, 1928.
Write direct to the hotel of your choice stating number of persons and kind
Any who are unable to secure accommodations should notify FRANK L. DE
Walnut Streets, Philadelphia.

[See other side for President's Letter

Coatesville, Pa.
May 25, 1928.

To the Members of the Association of Directo
of the Poor and Charities and Corrections
of Pennsylvania:

I realize in some degree the responsibilities devolving upon the Chairman of your
Association, and the difficulties which one
confronts in coming into a work of such magn
tude and such wide extent and importance.

I bespeak your indulgence and your co-operati
conduct of the work, and in the program of th
ciation to be held September 24th, to 27th, i
in Hotel, Philadelphia, (Chestnut Street at

ive Committee met in Philadelphia on April
pon a program, which I know you will find en-
ble.

ersonal letter and an invitation to you to re
make sure to come to the Convention.

s to be presented, I am sure you will find in
table, and some of the places around Philadel
visit you will find of especial interest.

any suggestions to offer, send them to the
JONES, 522 Washington Trust Building. Wash-
me, your President, and they will receive due
ration.

u for the honor you have conferred upon me an
rty co-operation,

Sincerely yours,

CHARLES L. HUSTON,
President

CPSIA information can be obtained
at www.ICGtesting.com
Printed in the USA
BVHW041001180119
538188BV00006B/96/P

9 780331 483246